FAIR LIBERTY'S
CALL

FAIR LIBERTY'S CALL

∾

Sharon Pollock

b broadview drama

NATIONAL LIBRARY OF CANADA CATALOGUING IN PUBLICATIONS DATA

Pollock, Sharon
       Fair liberty's call
       (Broadview drama)
       A play. Originally published: Toronto: Coach House Press 1995
       ISBN 1-55111-513-1
       1. United Empire Loyalists—Drama 2. United States—History—Revolution, 1775-1783. I. Title.

PS8581.O34F33 2002   C812'.54   C2001-904332-5
PR9199.3.P65F3 2002

Broadview Press Ltd. is an independent, international publishing house, incorporated in 1985. Broadview believes in shared ownership, both with its employees and with the general public; since the year 2000 Broadview shares have traded on the Toronto Venture Exchange under the symbol BDP.

We welcome comments and suggestions regarding any aspect of our publications—please feel free to contact us at the addresses below or at broadview@broadviewpress.com

Canada	*UK and Continental Europe*
Post Office Box 1243	Thomas Lyster Ltd.
Peterborough, Ontario	Units 3 and 4a, Old Boundary Way,
Canada K9J 7H5	Burscough Road, Ormskirk
Tel: (705) 743-8990	Lancashire L39 2YW, UK
Fax: (705) 743-8353	Tel: (01695) 575112; Fax: (01695) 570120
customerservice@broadviewpress.com	books@tlyster.co.uk
U.S.A.	*Australia*
3576 California Road	UNIREPS, University of New South Wales,
Orchard Park, NY 14127 USA	Sydney, NSW, Australia 2052
Tel: (705) 743-8990	Tel: 612 9664 0999
Fax: (705) 743-8353	Fax: 612 9664 5420
customerservice@broadviewpress.com	info.press@unsw.edu.au

www.broadviewpress.com

Broadview Press gratefully acknowledges the financial support of the Ministry of Canadian Heritage through the Book Publishing Industry Development Program.

❧

Book design by Lori Shyba, Sundial Media Ltd.
Front and back cover photography by Cylla von Tiedemann.
Courtesy of the Stratford Festival Archives.

Printed in Canada

INTRODUCTION

Fair Liberty's Call was commissioned by David William, Artistic Director of The Stratford Festival Theatre, and produced at The Tom Patterson Theatre under the direction of Guy Sprung.

The seed of the play, like all my work, is a question that haunts me. In the case of *Fair Liberty's Call* the question was: why are we the way we are? The "we" I was thinking of was not the "we" of Western Canada where I've spent most of my life. It was the Eastern Canadian "we," that of Upper Canada and the Maritimes where I was born and "grew up." I wondered what had birthed its establishment oligarchy and nurtured its ability to propagate the notion that the Canadian character is defined by peace, order and good government. This branding of identity was one Canadians from sea to shining sea were to model. I saw it (and still see it) as valuing legality over justice, passivity over action in the face of injustice or corruption, and traditional form over authentic content. It does not mirror the Western Canadian character as history has formed it, or as I know it. It is a model I didn't fit then, and still don't fit today.

While the seed or creative impulse for the play is the question, it is soon absorbed into the blood and bones of the characters, and the trappings of the plot. The question limits the growth of the play and is best forgotten. Characters take over. Their motivations and objectives, the finished play itself, reveals to me that when I asked myself "why are we the way we are?" it was not only a national or regional "we" my mind was toying with. The characters of Annie, Joan, and Eddie speak from the experience of another country, one not bound by geographic national borders, and one in which I do belong.

Some Historical Notes

1773 **BOSTON TEA PARTY:** American colonists dump tea shipments into Boston Harbour in protest of the tea tax, which the British Parliament has retained to demonstrate their taxing authority (without representation) over the American colonies.

1775 **LEXINGTON AND CONCORD:** The first open conflict of the American Revolution, when the British unsuccessfully attempt to seize ammunition stores from the Americans, and to arrest the leader of The Boston Tea Party.

1775 **BUNKER HILL:** A costly British victory that actually takes place on Breeder's Hill.

1775 **QUEBEC CITY:** Benedict Arnold distinguishes himself leading American militia in an unsuccessful bid to draw British forces from New England by attacking Quebec.

1776 **LONG ISLAND:** Unsuccessful attack by the Americans leads to their defeat at White Plains and British seizure of Fort Washington.

1777 **BRANDYWINE:** A British tactical success that fails to deter the Revolution.

1777 **SARATOGA:** A series of battles ending in final defeat for British forces, in which Benedict Arnold's American militia plays a key role; it is a turning point in the war leading to France's decision to provide aid to the Rebels.

1778 **MONMOUTH:** Neither side claims success but a moral victory for the Americans.

1778 **CHERRY VALLEY:** Butler's Rangers and Indian allies massacre American settlers.

1779 A year of skirmishes and battles ending with the Siege of Savannah.

1780	Benedict Arnold, perhaps feeling his contribution to the war effort is insufficiently acknowledged, offers to sell the plans of West Point to the British. Major John Andre, acting as Britain's liaison with Arnold, is captured with incriminating papers outside of Tarrytown, and subsequently hanged.
1780	CHARLESTON: A British victory and major setback for American forces.
1780	CAMDEN: A disastrous American loss with the American general fleeing the battlefield and Banastre Tarleton hailed as a national hero in Britain.
1780	WAXHAWS: Tarleton's Legion overtakes and defeats Americans as they retreat after the fall of Charleston. Also known as Buford's Massacre.
1780	KING'S MOUNTAIN: An American victory, destroying the British army's left wing.
1781	COWPENS: Tarleton's Legion soundly defeated by the Americans, again a turning point in favour of the Revolution.
1781	GUILDFORD COURT HOUSE: A major British loss foreshadowing Yorktown.
1781	YORKTOWN: Fighting ends with the British surrendering to General Washington and his American and French forces, in effect the end of the war.
1781-83	New York population triples as Loyalists flee there to escape personal danger after legal looting of their property. A group of fifty-five petition for special treatment in Canadian land allotment to ensure they regain their former status in society.

1783	"Provincials" (men from Loyalist regiments and their families, including the fifty-five) and "refugees" (civilian Loyalist individuals and families) are transported by fleets of ships to Nova Scotia, and what will become New Brunswick.
1784	*The Saint John Gazette* prints an anonymous letter signed "A Soldier" attacking preferential treatment of the fifty-five in land and supplies allotment. A second letter leads to a conviction for libel, the fining of the paper's publishers, and the *Gazette's* demise.
1785	Candidates representing the fifty-five fail in their bid for election to the newly-created New Brunswick assembly. Governor Carleton approves the scrutinizing of all ballots resulting in the disallowing of sufficient votes to allow the election of the fifty-five's slate of candidates. "An Act Against Tumults and Disorders" is passed, banning petitioning (the most popular form of political action), and, in effect, banning free speech in New Brunswick.

❧

"TO GIVE QUARTER" . . .To promise not to kill an enemy soldier who is surrendering. A soldier may ask for and may be given quarter.

"CONTINENTALS" . . . . .Trained and uniformed soldiers of the American army, not local militia.

"BRITISH LEGION" . . . . .A fighting unit made up of infantry and mounted troops.

"HESSIANS" . . . . .German mercenaries who fought for the British.

❧

~

BANASTRE TARLETON, born in 1754, a graduate of Oxford,
purchased a rank in the military in 1775 and at twenty-three was
promoted to Lieutenant Colonel in the British Legion serving in
America. His reliance on speed and surprise, strategic use of
infantry and cavalry, and his leadership in battle led to success on
the field and the admiration of his men. The enemy was said to
panic at the mere sight of the green jackets of Tarleton's Legion.
Hailed as a hero after his success at Camden, he became infamous
at the Waxhaws when he and his men continued to attack
American forces who laid down their arms asking for "quarter."
"Tarleton's quarter," meaning no quarter, became the rallying cry
of the Americans when they met up with his Legion at the
Cowpens. Here Tarleton suffered a crushing defeat and barely
escaped with his life. Although successful military engagements
followed, his reputation was coloured by the events at Waxhaws
and Cowpens. He and his Legion surrendered at Yorktown. When
American officers hosted the defeated British officers at dinner, no
American invited Tarleton to his table and none would sit with
him, because, he was told, of his past atrocities. Nevertheless he
returned to England as a hero, was promoted to general, was
knighted, and served in the British Parliament, dying in 1833.

Sharon Pollock
Calgary
June 2002

Above: Scene from the 1993 Stratford Festival production of *Fair Liberty's Call.* Directed by Guy Sprung. Designed by Maryse Bienvenu with left to right: Michael Hogan as George Roberts, Janet Wright as Joan Roberts, Kristina Nicholl as Annie Roberts and Philippa Domville as Eddie Roberts. Photographed by Cylla von Tiedemann. Courtesy of the Stratford Festival Archives.

Front Cover: Scene from the 1993 Stratford Festival production of *Fair Liberty's Call* with Tyrone Benskin as Wullie. Photographed by Cylla von Tiedemann. Courtesy of the Stratford Festival Archives.

Back Cover: Scene from the 1993 Stratford Festival production of *Fair Liberty's Call* with foreground left to right: Tyrone Benskin as Wullie and Ted Dykstra as Daniel Wilson, and background left to right: Philippa Domville as Eddie Roberts, Michael Hogan as George Roberts and Wayne Best as John Anderson. Photographed by Cylla von Tiedemann. Courtesy of the Stratford Festival Archives.

PREMIERE PRODUCTION

Fair Liberty's Call was first produced by the Stratford Festival in the Tom Patterson Theatre, July 10 to August 28, 1993, with the following cast:

JOAN ROBERTS:	Janet Wright
ANNIE ROBERTS:	Kristina Nicoll
EDDIE ROBERTS:	Philippa Domville
GEORGE ROBERTS:	Michael Hogan
MAJOR ABIJAH WILLIAMS:	David Ferry
DANIEL WILSON:	Ted Dykstra
MAJOR JOHN ANDERSON:	Wayne Best
WULLIE:	Tyrone Benskin

∿

DIRECTOR:	Guy Sprung
COSTUME DESIGNER:	Maryse Bienvenu
MUSIC COMPOSED BY:	R. Bill Gagnon and Geneviève Maufette
LIGHTING DESIGNER:	Kevin Fraser
SOUND DESIGNER:	Evan Turner
CHOREOGRAPHER:	John Broome
FIGHT DIRECTOR:	John Stead
STAGE MANAGER:	Janet Sellery
ASSISTANT STAGE MANAGERS:	Bruno Gonsalves and Theresa Malek
PRODUCTION STAGE MANAGER:	Catherine Russell
ASSISTANT DIRECTOR:	Paulina B. Abarca
ASSISTANT LIGHTING DESIGNER:	Bonnie Beecher
FIGHT CAPTAIN:	Wayne Best

PERSONS

JOAN ROBERTS
Late 50s.

ANNIE ROBERTS
Joan's daughter, in her mid-20s.

EDDIE ROBERTS
Joan's second daughter, in her early 20s, who has dressed and lived as a man since she was 16. She is an ex-captain in Tarleton's English Legion, a Loyalist unit in the American Revolution.

GEORGE ROBERTS
Husband of Joan and father of Annie and Eddie, mid-60s.

MAJOR ABIJAH WILLIAMS
Mid-40s, formerly a major in Tarleton's Legion.

DANIEL WILSON
Mid-20s, ex-corporal in the Legion.

MAJOR JOHN ANDERSON
Early 30s, also a Major.

WULLIE
Early 30s, former scout with the Legion.

PLACE

NEW BRUNSWICK

TIME

1785

IN THE OPENING SEGMENT, characters speak to the audience as well as to each other. They have a compelling need to tell; to tell before someone else tells; to correct a former mistelling; to tell before they're unable to tell, or prevented from telling. This doesn't mean they are rushed, although they may be intense. They may agree or disagree; they may harbour good or ill feelings, feel defensive or proud regarding past actions or inactions—their own or others'—as revealed in the telling. They may find some amusement in their past and present.

All sound is impressionistic, even surrealistic, rather than realistic.

ACT ONE

> (*A faint majestic orchestral version of* God Save the King *is heard. Lights reveal the characters on stage, but not yet into, or intruding on, the space, a bare stage, the floor of which radiates in a dark-hued swirl of colour. Although this space appears empty and uncorrupted, it projects an aura of foreboding, a sense of the unseen.* JOAN *and* ANNIE *each carry a large bundle of belongings,* EDDIE *carries a long gun,* WULLIE *is somewhat isolated but not far from* EDDIE, DANIEL *stands between the shafts of a wagon, one in each hand, ready to pull. It is piled high with barrels, trunks and rough pieces of wood.* GEORGE *has a trunk lashed to his back and carries a keg.* MAJOR WILLIAMS, DANIEL *and* WULLIE *carry long guns. The characters are still but not "frozen."*
>
> God Save the King, *which has started well, continues for a bit but then grows increasingly distorted, fragmenting, chaotic. The anthem crossfades with, and is overtaken by, the sound of a horrific battle, gunfire and cannon, men*

yelling encouragement and despair mixed with the cries of the wounded and the thunder and screams of horses. The anthem is gone and the battle din grows increasingly loud, deafeningly loud. It stops. Silence.

JOAN, ANNIE and EDDIE step slowly into the space. As they speak, the swirl of dark colours on the stage floor is gradually supplanted by dappled light evoking a glade in a stand of hardwood trees with sunlight filtering through the leaves. They speak over a taped montage of their own voices repeating the following words with some resonance.)

JOAN:	*You want to know where*
ANNIE:	*where*
JOAN:	*where to put your eye*
ANNIE:	*eye*
JOAN:	*eye so you can hear the*
ANNIE:	*heart*
JOAN:	*beat*
ANNIE:	*heartbeat*
JOAN:	*heartbeat*
ANNIE:	*of a country*
JOAN:	*country comin' into*
ANNIE:	*country*
JOAN:	*comin' into*
ANNIE:	*country comin' into*
EDDIE:	*country comin' into bein'*

(The characters slowly begin to inhabit the space. WULLIE hangs back. Squatting on the back of her heels, EDDIE takes a crumpled piece of paper from her pocket and flattens it out carefully. It has blood on it. She wipes the blood on the front of her jacket, notices she has blood on her hand and rubs it into the fabric with her palm. Then she checks to assure herself that the blood is gone. She carefully folds the paper and places it in her pocket as ANNIE puts her bundle down and wipes her forehead.)

JOAN: When first we come here after the revolution, when first we come.... I saw a woman in the woods. A red woman. I saw her watchin'. Watchin' with a babe on her back. I saw her carryin' it like that, like—packed in moss, like—like nothin' I know. One mornin' I found a feather on the doorstep.

ANNIE: We don't have a doorstep, Mama. We haven't had a doorstep since Boston. We may never have a doorstep again.

JOAN: The feather was there. And in the sky a bird was circlin'. A bird like no bird I know. The colours were wrong, and the size. It circled three times. Three times. Then it soared up, up, wings outstretched, but not movin' its wings .... This is a barren place. This wasn't home, isn't home, is no place I know, no, no place I know.

(GEORGE moves further into the space, places the trunk and keg on the stage and gets out a neatly folded English flag. EDDIE assists him in guiding a white birchbark pole into place so the English flag may be attached and flown from this makeshift flagpole.)

GEORGE: If you wanna know, I'll tell ya. Me, I'm George Roberts, formerly of Boston and one of that city's foremost citizens and merchants. And I never supported the Rebels! I lost every penny I had strugglin' against those traitors. I remained true to the King and to Parliament, and I lost everything, and I end up here with nothin'! To get somethin', I need to get in with the Committee of Fifty-five Families. Major Abijah Williams is the agent for the Fifty-five; Major Williams served with the Loyalist Legion; Major Williams fought with Eddie and I think he's hot on my daughter Annie. Do you see where I'm goin' with this? Eh, Eddie?

(EDDIE walks away from her father.)

Eddie!

JOAN:	Father (*indicating* GEORGE *with her right thumb*). Mother (*indicating herself with her right forefinger*). Four. Four Children (*extending four fingers of her left hand*). Home (*her right hand folded into a fist*).
ANNIE:	We're home now, Mama. New Brunswick is home.
JOAN:	Four Children, Father, Mother, Richard, Annie, Em'ly, Edward, Home!

JOAN:
There was a table, a little table—there—in the parlour—and a sofa, there—and a whatnot in the parlour, yes! And a chair! Over there—and another one there! And it was all in a kind of maroon, a red, crimson red, a deep, dark red, and it was all—There was a rug! It was red! And a—

ANNIE:
Hush…. He was nineteen. Richard, my older brother? Nineteen when he died. And Edward? My younger brother Edward? Killed himself at the farm in Tarrytown. That's a fact and we're dealin' in facts, aren't we? And Em'ly? My sister Em'ly?

EDDIE:
Now if you be a Rebel-owned slave and you run away and fight for the Loyalists, you'd be freed by the Loyalists.

WULLIE:
(*Moving further into the space.*) But if you did the same thing, and was Loyalist-owned, you wouldn't be freed, no sir. Fightin' for the Loyalists won't buy my freedom 'less I be a run-away Rebel-owned slave.

EDDIE:
Before Wullie could join the Exodus out of New York after we lost the war he had to prove he'd been Rebel-owned and that he wasn't no run-away Loyalist slave.

WULLIE:
If I could prove that, I'd get my certificate, a certificate sayin' I was a free Coloured, sayin' I could join the Exodus, and sayin' I was eligible for land.

EDDIE:
Wullie fought as a scout with Tarleton's Loyalist Legion. Wullie saved my life, but Wullie couldn't prove he was a Rebel-owned slave, could have been owned by a Loyalist … so … what're you going to do?…. Proof be hard to come by. And without proof, Wullie can't get no certificate.

Wullie needs a certificate.

(*DANIEL pulls the wagon further into the space. With*

EDDIE and THE MAJOR, he will alter and further delineate the space, taking from the wagon additional items to sit or stand on.)

DANIEL: Whipped! I don't mind sayin' it. We got our Loyalist ass whipped by the Rebel Delaware Continentals. I thought we'd killed or taken 'em all at the battle of Camden but there they were, those Rebel boys turnin' up again as we come 'round the cowpens and Benny Tarleton, as he swings onto his horse, he says, he says "Kill every Rebel prisoner!" *(laughs)* Hell, we didn't take no prisoners! We were damn lucky we weren't taken as prisoners, eh Major?

MAJOR: Do you remember Colonel Tarleton leadin' the charge, Daniel? His reins in his left hand, his right arm in a sling, and no way to draw either gun or his sabre!

DANIEL: I'd have followed him into the gates of Hell. Eh, Eddie?

EDDIE: We did.

DANIEL: You know, to think on it now, seems like kind of a foolish thing for him to have done.

MAJOR: Courageous! Not foolish, courageous!

DANIEL: He could have been killed.

MAJOR: That's what makes it courageous.

DANIEL: I wonder what he was thinkin' of doin' when he got into the thick of things, and him with only one useful hand and that hand on the reins.

MAJOR: Do what he did do—charge with no means of defendin' himself! Lead his own men into battle with a cry on his lips. "Come on my boys! Huzzaaaa!"

DANIEL: "Huzzaaaa!" he says!

MAJOR: "Ride like Hell!"

DANIEL: "And shoot like devils!"

EDDIE: "And take no prisoners."

(The sound of a whistle is heard, two notes rising and falling, birdlike, followed by a dry rattle. EDDIE, DANIEL and THE MAJOR share a flask, then rest a while from their labours.)

JOAN:	That is not Edward! *(Indicating EDDIE)* Edward is dead!
ANNIE:	That's right, Mama, he's dead.
JOAN:	Edward and Em'ly, both of them gone! Only seven minutes between them. Yes, my belly was big, and the two of them, they'd kick and tussle in there, and I'd sit, put my hands on my belly like this, and I'd feel them, kickin' in there. I'd sit in the parlour, ooohhh it was a wonderful room, it was all ... and ... and, Edward came home ...
GEORGE:	Stop her.
JOAN:	then where were we livin'? not livin' in Boston
ANNIE:	How am I supposed to do that?
JOAN:	burnt outa Boston
GEORGE:	It's past, it's gone, Mama!
JOAN:	and not here yet
ANNIE:	Let her go. Get it over with.
JOAN:	Tarrytown! Livin' at the farm in Tarrytown! And Edward came home from—from where did he come from?
ANNIE:	Cherry Valley.
JOAN:	And the Loyalist Rangers and he lay on the bed and his eyes, what were his eyes?
ANNIE:	They were open.
JOAN:	And the pistol was where?
ANNIE:	On the table beside the bed.
JOAN:	And he wasn't the same. Sixteen he was—and—"He can't go back" I said to his father.
GEORGE:	Edward would do what was right.
JOAN:	Edward would do what his father wanted, that's what Edward would do, what he always did.
GEORGE:	Do what he wanted.
JOAN:	I was out in the hall when I heard it and as soon as I heard it I knew. I'd known since the day he came home. All that time I'd been waitin' to hear it. First the noise, and after the noise, the sound of a gun as it fell to the floor. A small kind of noise, not like the other, and then ... no noise at

	all. I stood there ... holdin' my breath, not breathin' ... and knowin' ... we ...
ANNIE:	Buried him.
JOAN:	We buried Edward and we said—
ANNIE:	It was Em'ly. We said it was my sister Em'ly.
JOAN:	Isn't that what we said? We said it was Em'ly. Dead. Of the smallpox. That's what we said. And Em'ly? She picked up Edward's gun—
GEORGE:	She wanted to do it!
JOAN:	—put on Edward's jacket, cut off her hair, joined the Legion, Tarleton's Loyalist Legion, Bloody Banastre Tarleton's Bloody Loyalist Legion! Because! Her father said!
GEORGE:	Because it was necessary!
JOAN:	It was Necessary! Because of Richard! Their Rebel Brother, our Son! Because of their Loyalist father! Because of you! Because of King and country and taxes and tea and—!
GEORGE:	It does no good. Hush, Mama!
JOAN:	And Annie was there when you drove Richard out.
ANNIE:	I was there in the hallway.
GEORGE:	Annie, please.
JOAN:	And Em'ly and Edward at the top of the stairs and all of them watchin' their own father drive their own brother out, drive Richard out! And he went!
ANNIE:	But he stopped.
JOAN:	At the end of the walk. And he turned. Even then I don't think he'd have gone, but his father, he slammed the door. I ran to the window. Richard saw me—saw me there at the window—and he just lifted his hand in a bit of a wave— then he turned—and he went. My son Richard, who signed with the Rebels. My son! Son of liberty! Country, King, taxes and tea and round and round the Liberty Tree! Patriot Son!
ANNIE:	They're called Rebels, Mama.

JOAN: But the English, they caught him, caught Richard. They had him with the Patriot prisoners packed and freezin' and starvin' in the holds of the English ships. Winter, and them in the holds below the water line in the East River! I begged! Good Loyalist man like your father? "Go to New York! Get leniency for Richard!" He could have done it. I begged! He wouldn't. I begged, and he wouldn't.

ANNIE: Here are the facts—Papa was for representation in the English Parliament; Richard for separation and independence. And they fought, first each other, and then ... It's true he was taken, held in the Long Island Prison Ships, and then—there was a prisoner exchange and later he died, we were told, in one of the battles they called Saratoga where he fought under Arnold. *(smiles)* That's right. Benedict Arnold. That's not fiction, that's fact. *(laughs)* He served under Benedict Arnold. Second time 'cause he served under Arnold at the Siege of Quebec. My Rebel brother served under Benedict Arnold. Isn't that funny?

JOAN: That's when he sent Edward—him—*(indicating GEORGE)* her father sent Edward, he was only fifteen but he made him sign up!

GEORGE: Edward wanted to go!

JOAN: Edward signed with the Loyalist Rangers, went scalpin' and killin' all through the Valley, red Cherry Valley! His father thought that was going to balance things out! Richard there, Richard there, one Rebel son, and then poor Edward, the Loyalist son. And when Edward died, make Em'ly go! Turn her into Edward. Turn her into Eddie. Eddie take Richard take Edward take Emily Three! Three of them gone! *(to EDDIE)* Murderer! You're a murderer!

(DANIEL, EDDIE and THE MAJOR resume transforming the space.)

MAJOR: Cowan Ford!

DANIEL: Cowan Ford!

MAJOR: Cowan Ford as we was crossin' to the far bank!

DANIEL: And the Rebels was firin' on us hot and heavy!

MAJOR : Horses snortin' and us all hollerin' and drownin' and dyin'! *(laughs)* You remember that, Eddie?

DANIEL: I'm going to tell you somethin'. At Cowan Ford I seen Frank Taylor—I seen him—there was this here Rebel boy firin' at us and he fell into the water from off of the bank they was firin' from—and the current got him. And Frank knew him, he knew him, he recognized him like. And Frank he hollers, "Billy boy!" he says. "Billy boy, it's me!" And he holds out his hand like so? The Rebel boy, he looks up from the water, and he finds his footin', and he starts splashin' and wadin' towards us, reachin' out towards Frank. He reaches out for Frank's hand. And Frank, he ups with his gun and he fires.

MAJOR: I never seen that.

EDDIE: I seen it.

DANIEL: And the Rebel boy he fell back, and the river took him. Took him, and the horses, and our red-coated dead. The river took 'em all. They floated away. *(Pause)* Ah, what the hell. We're here. It's a bloody miracle, but we're here. We may've lost everything, but we're here. Yaaaaa-Hoo!

MAJOR: Huzzaa!

MAJOR AND DANIEL: *(Singing as they leave the space)*

> *If ... buttercups buzzed after the bee*
> *If boats ... were on land, churches on sea*
>
>> *(Under the song voices call out to each other randomly: on top of each other, far off, remote, echoing, faint, resonating, mixed with the faint sound of gunfire "Huzzaa!" "Come on my boys!" "Remember the Cowpens!" "Ride like Hell!" "Shoot like devils!" "Billy boy, this way, Billy boy!")*
>
> *If ... ponies rode men and grass ate the cow*
> *If summer were spring and the other way 'round*
> *Then ... all of the world ... would be upside down!*

(*WULLIE follows DANIEL off. THE MAJOR stops and remains on the periphery in the shadows. EDDIE watches them leave. They seem to disappear into a smudge of smoke that drifts from the upstage periphery of the space. The gunfire and voices resonate and fade as JOAN speaks.*)

JOAN: Up in the woods where I saw the red woman, there are bones. Leg bones of a man, maybe a man.... Arm bones. Part of a Rib Cage, and a Skull missin' the Jaw. Disarranged. When you stand there, you feel your feet restin' on top of the soil. You could slip. You could fall. Empty eyesockets catch your eye tellin' you somethin'. Your feet carry you back to the house but they leave no trace of your passing.... This isn't home. They aren't our Dead. The red woman stands in the glade of trees, and she watches.

(*A faint bird call followed by a dry rattle heard at random intervals as EDDIE jumps up on the wagon and speaks addressing a crowd.*)

EDDIE: Hear this! If you be a Loyalist, colonial born, and you fought for the English, and you got taken by Rebels, you'd not be exchanged, for the English accepted the Rebels' namin' you as a traitor. But if you fought for the English and you be English born, and got taken by Rebels, you could be freed. English-born soldier for Rebel soldier, in a one-for-one prisoner exchange. Colonial born you could rot in a Rebel prison. What does that tell you?

I served as a soldier, Loyalist soldier, colonial born, bloodied my hands and my arms, waded in gore, in the name of a King who condoned his enemies' namin' me traitor. What does that tell you?

Now, after the revolution, the Loyalist soldier was promised land. Land and material goods to start fresh in this new place. Our reward for remainin' loyal to the King. Three years later, the Loyalist soldier is still waitin' for that reward. Instead of it, we get absentee landlords, with the best land given to those who already have power and pride and position! The ordinary soldier, like you or like me, gets a remote or barren plot—or no plot at all! Or he must submit to be a tenant and farm for the absentee landlord! What does that tell you?

And now those same who abuse us, and I'll name them— the Committee of Fifty-five Families—have put up a slate of candidates for election to office in the Assembly! What does that tell you?

Here's news, friends. There's opposition to the Fifty-five, and that opposition is mounting a slate of alternate candidates! What does that tell you? Exercise freedom of choice, citizens, or be party to your own oppression!

(The sound of the dry rattle. It stops.)

Signed. "A Soldier."

EDDIE moves out of the space.

GEORGE:	Today is October 22nd, 1785!
JOAN:	What day's today?
GEORGE:	Today is a Day for Rememberin'!
JOAN:	Is that today?
GEORGE:	Four years ago today is the Day the World Turned Upside Down!
JOAN:	Today?
GEORGE:	The Day Yorktown fell!
JOAN:	That's not today.
GEORGE:	The Day we Lost the War!
JOAN:	Day we lost.
GEORGE:	So there's Reunion tonight! And Rememberin'! And Tarleton Legion Merry-makin'! And business tonight!

END OF OPENING SEGMENT, NO BREAK IN DIALOGUE OR ACTION

ANNIE:	Look, I've burnt my hand twice and singed my eyebrows and the front of my hair tendin' the porker for this bloody reunion. *(A faint thunder-like sound rumbles.)* Rain—and now the coals in the pit'll go out, and we can all have pink porker, won't that be nice.
JOAN:	*(Sitting alone, at a distance from the other characters. She is engaged in repetitious slicing of bread, cheese and sausage. Her voice is a faint murmur under the dialogue.)*
	Pink porker, pink porker, pink porker.
ANNIE:	What's that?

(GEORGE is opening the keg.)

GEORGE:	Rum. The Major's here, and he's provided the rum. Where's the Legion standard? Eddie should've had it up and planted before dark.
ANNIE:	Is it dark? *(It isn't.)*
GEORGE:	You have a way with you, girl. I hope you marry a man with restraint. He'll need it.
ANNIE:	Who should I marry?

(GEORGE is searching for the Legion standard.)

GEORGE:	Abijah Williams. *(Annie laughs.)* Humour an old man, it's not such a bad idea.
ANNIE:	It's a terrible idea. Don't ever have it.
GEORGE:	He's in thick with the Fifty-five, and they're the ones to be thick with if you want to thrive in this neck of the woods.

(MAJOR WILLIAMS' attention is on GEORGE and ANNIE.)

ANNIE:	Amongst other voids and vacuums of character, he is totally lacking in restraint—and well you know it.

(GEORGE finds the Legion standard.)

GEORGE:	Where's Eddie?
ANNIE:	Not here. *(The sound of the wind is heard. The light flickers.)* There'll be nobody come in this weather.
GEORGE:	Them that can come will come, and Eddie should be here to greet them.

(GEORGE exits with the standard.)

ANNIE: When you're finished take a look at the porker! Build up the coals under the porker!

MAJOR: *(Approaching ANNIE.)* Porker is it?

ANNIE: That's right, Major. When Papa heard there were pigs at the neighbours, over he went and brought into play every bargainin' trick learnt in a lifetime of buyin' and sellin' the Empire's tea.

MAJOR: Roast pig.

(He savours the words as he eyes ANNIE; ANNIE will draw him a rum during the following.)

ANNIE: He was determined. I think he'd heard roast pig was your favourite.

MAJOR: And not too easy to come by.

ANNIE: He'd have sold his soul for it, though I believe that went in exchange for the tent our first winter here. Or on some other occasion of need. Or demand. *(ANNIE gives THE MAJOR a rum.)* To kill the last of the chill from your ride.

MAJOR: It was a bone-chilling ride. It may take a bit more than the rum.

(He grabs ANNIE. She struggles to free herself. JOAN is still sitting alone, preparing the food. She watches.)

JOAN: Like a bullet-hole in the head! Like a rope catchin' you under the chin! Like a narrow ravine, a depression, a dip—like a Valley! Like saltwater runnin' out of the bay, like the tide rushin' into the gorge!

(ANNIE manages to hit THE MAJOR back-handed across the face with her clenched fist, not a slap. The blow gives him pause. The sleeve of ANNIE's blouse is ripped, exposing her arm. GEORGE returning catches the end of the confrontation.)

GEORGE: The... coals are banked, and the spit's turned.

ANNIE: And isn't it a terrible job? It's a terrible dangerous job for a woman. I've been at it all day, and the smell of roast pig and cracklin' has so permeated my clothin' that the Major here has just fallen on me as if I were a chop. Isn't that right Major? *(He smiles and takes a drink of rum. ANNIE extends her arm to her father.)* Smell.

GEORGE: Get me rum like a good girl, eh. *(ANNIE gives GEORGE his rum and withdraws a bit, observing the men as she assists JOAN.)* What've you heard from the Fifty-five?

MAJOR: Be better if Eddie were here.

GEORGE: Why Eddie?

MAJOR: The greater part of the cash you'll see in a year is Eddie's half-pay captain's pension, and your largest allotment's his acreage for Loyalist Legion service. Don't that give him a say in the matter?

GEORGE: We're talkin' land allotment to members of the Fifty-five Families, and that's got nothin' to do with military service or rank.

MAJOR: You forget, George. You're not a member of the Fifty-five.

(As GEORGE speaks, THE MAJOR removes a newspaper, the Gazette, *from his pocket.)*

GEORGE But I support them, don't I? And I support their Assembly slate for election. All I ask is greater land allotment as material recognition of my former position and loss as a citizen loyal to the Crown! You and I know the only real money to be had in this country is land. Land is money and money's land.

MAJOR: Have you read the *Gazette?*

GEORGE: The *Gazette!* Why do you ask?

MAJOR: There's an interestin' letter in the *Gazette.*

(He passes the paper to GEORGE to read.)

Read it.

(EDDIE enters. THE MAJOR, seeing EDDIE, raises his rum in a toast that EDDIE acknowledges with a nod, as GEORGE

continues to read the Gazette. **EDDIE** *draws a drink of rum.*)

To Tarleton's Legion—How many of the boys do you think'll make it?

EDDIE:	Some. Fewer than last year.
MAJOR:	Have you read the *Gazette*? (**EDDIE** *nods.*) Interestin' letter in the *Gazette*.
EDDIE:	You think so, eh.
MAJOR:	The man who delivered it to the paper, as well as the printer? They've both been charged.
EDDIE:	With what?
MAJOR:	Seditious and scandalous libel. You'll note the article carries no name, it's simply signed "A Soldier." Of course the author's identity is known.
EDDIE:	I wrote it.
MAJOR:	The matter'll be carried no further, as regards legal action 'gainst that individual, given certain assurances.
EDDIE:	We've been robbed of our rights.

(**GEORGE** *crumples up the paper and throws it down.* **ANNIE** *will retrieve it unobtrusively when she gets the chance, smooth it out, and read it.*)

GEORGE:	That's enough Eddie!
EDDIE:	The best lots in town and country are reserved for particular persons, those bein' the Committee of Fifty-five Families.
GEORGE:	Whose position and placement warrant it!
EDDIE:	My father and me have been cheated and robbed in the matter of land, buildin' materials and clothin' owin' to us for my Loyalist service.
GEORGE:	I'm seein' to that!
EDDIE:	Is that theft now to extend to freedom of speech?
GEORGE:	That (*the* Gazette) is incitement to rebellion, that's what it is. You'd have to be blind not to see it, and a fool to write it!

MAJOR:	Listen, Eddie, your land registration could be expedited and your allotment expanded, some indentured persons could be made available—
EDDIE:	Slaves you mean.
MAJOR:	Indentured persons made available—if you could make available any information you have regarding—
EDDIE:	Inform, you mean.
GEORGE:	Listen to him, Eddie.
EDDIE:	I acted alone.
MAJOR:	We know there's division in the populace as regards the election and the Fifty-five's slate for Assembly, so any information you might come across regardin' alternate candidates and their strategy would be welcome, that's all I'm sayin'.
EDDIE:	Quick—who does he remind you of?
GEORGE:	It's an opportunity, Eddie.
EDDIE:	The Rebels' Safety Committee in Boston, isn't that it? That band of vigilantes and hoodlums? I remember when they demanded allegiance to the Rebel Congress you swore allegiance to the Rebel Congress and the Royal Crown. And at the same time you denied allegiance to both Royal Crown and Rebel Congress, and all so eloquently done it prevented you gettin' tarred. Of course they eventually sorted it out and burnt our house! But, by then we were well on our way to Tarrytown. Still, better our house than your hide, eh? But—I almost forgot—Major Williams here has his own Rebel Committee of Safety experience. Unfortunately he was not so eloquent in bestridin' two worlds, and I understand you lost two toes to a tarrin', sir.
MAJOR:	I was eloquent alright. The smell of bubblin' tar makes a man eloquent. What I lacked was a son in the Rebel army!
GEORGE:	I had no son with the Rebels! I cut that boy out of my heart, and if it takes a tarrin' to show the world that, then I'd welcome a tarrin'! I have Eddie, and Eddie is foolish and simple and easily led!

(THE MAJOR moves to replenish his rum. GEORGE follows him.)

Eddie may give the appearance of a man, he may wield the gun and the sabre like a man, but Eddie needs guidance.

(The sound of Revolutionary Tea played on a recorder.)

Eddie will do whatever's required!

(Sound of DANIEL, gun slung over his shoulder, drunk, having fun, keeping time to the recorder with "HutZa! HutZa!" as he marches.)

For God's sake let's not leave it there!

(DANIEL, enter. Behind him is JOHN ANDERSON who is playing the recorder and has a long gun slung over his shoulder.)

DANIEL: Huzza! Huzza! Yuh! *(Stops)*

(ANDERSON stops playing.)

JOAN: Play.

DANIEL: Corporal Daniel Wilson! At your service and ready for grog, sir!

MAJOR: Corporal.

DANIEL: That's the Major—*(taking EDDIE's rum)* And here's me, Captain! Thank you, Eddie. And there's the pure sweet angel I been tellin' you about, ain't she a dream? You're a dream, Annie. I'm going to kiss the hem of your dress 'cause you're a dream and an angel!

(He gets down to do so. ANNIE pushes him over with the toe of her boot.)

ANNIE: You're drunk, Daniel Wilson.

DANIEL: Of course I'm drunk. How the hell's a man to keep the blood in his veins from freezin' in this new land if he don't mix it with a bit of grog? It's a life-savin' measure, sweet Annie. Now! I want you all to meet—this here friend of mine—this—What did you say your name was?

ANDERSON: Anderson.

DANIEL: Anderson! And I met him like this! I'm comin' along the road there and I see him just off to the side shelterin' under some trees, like.

ANDERSON: That's right.

DANIEL: No grog, you see, so the cold was just creepin' into his bones. God, but you're beautiful, girl. When you boarded the Exodus ship, and Eddie says "This is my sister," my heart beat like it never beat in six years of war. I got a good lot, Annie, it runs to the river—

EDDIE: Is it registered?

DANIEL: That'll come, Eddie, stay out of this. It's the last winter I'll spend in a tent. Will you marry me, Annie? (*ANNIE laughs and shakes her head "no."*) She's beautiful, isn't she? And her father is beautiful too! A beautiful man.

JOAN: (*Sings to ANDERSON*)
Hi says the little leather winged bat
I'll tell you the reason that

DANIEL: And this

JOAN: *The reason that I sing in the night*

DANIEL: is her mother.

JOAN: *Is because I lost my heart's delight*

ANNIE: That's enough, Mama. (*drawing her away*)

DANIEL: Where was I?

ANDERSON: I was told I'd find lodgin' if I kept to the road.

DANIEL: Whoever told you that's crazier than a hoot owl.

ANDERSON: So it seems.

DANIEL: So I said to him, him, under the trees there, I said, "Are you a military man?" "Yes," says he. So I says, "There's a few of the boys from Tarleton's Legion gatherin' tonight, and if George Roberts don't make you welcome, and the boys don't open their arms to a fellow soldier, then I'm George Washington's cat. So what do you say, eh? ... (*pause*) Meow?

GEORGE: I'm—sorry—welcome, I say welcome—more rum, Annie.

ANDERSON:	Thank you, sir.
MAJOR:	Anderson, eh?
ANNIE:	Where did you serve?
ANDERSON:	The Loyalist Rangers, ma'am.
MAJOR:	Rank?
ANDERSON:	Major.
MAJOR:	Ah.
JOAN:	*(to ANDERSON)* Edward?
GEORGE:	Hush.
DANIEL:	Eddie served with the Loyalist Rangers 'fore Tarleton's Legion. Right, Eddie?
ANDERSON:	*(to EDDIE)* Prior to my enlistment perhaps.
EDDIE:	Perhaps.
DANIEL:	Where's the bits and pieces?
GEORGE:	We was just gettin' to that.
DANIEL:	How the hell's a man to remember with no surroundin's?

(MAJOR WILLIAMS, GEORGE and DANIEL begin to drag out the totems, souvenirs, and trophies of war from trunks, boxes and containers. They will decorate both the space and themselves as they prepare for the Remembrance Ritual. EDDIE observes more than she assists, lending a hand when needed. An American Rebel flag is draped over a makeshift table. A large picture of King George will be raised to oversee the proceedings. The regimental drum and sticks, their Tarleton green uniforms, an elaborately embroidered, but stained, waistcoat, a uniform jacket with lace epaulettes stiff with stains, an iron helmet, a black leather cap with a white skull and the words "Or Glory" on it as well as various regimental flags and colours are all displayed.)

DANIEL:	Gotta fill the place up with things that speak of the past.
MAJOR:	Else how's a man to know who he is?

(JOAN approaches ANDERSON, ANNIE follows her.)

JOAN:	Edward served with the Rangers.
ANNIE:	Edward hadn't the stomach for scalpin' so he left the Rangers, eh Mama?
ANDERSON:	If it's scalp or be scalped, you can't blame a man for scalpin', ma'am.
ANNIE:	Was that the choice?

(ANDERSON shifts away from the women to the men.)

DANIEL:	Lookey here! Lookey lookey here! *(He holds up a Tarleton green jacket and throws Eddie a second green jacket; they're dirty and well worn.)* Legion green for the occasion, and rookie see *(holding up his foot)* the best pair of boots I ever owned. Get your green on, Eddie.
MAJOR:	You're still wearin' those boots?
DANIEL:	These boots got a history, Major. I took 'em off a Rebel, but a fella I know says they're English boots these boots, so that Rebel stole 'em off an English corpse—and I stole 'em off of the Rebel's corpse—so what do you say, eh? Round and round, eh, Major?
MAJOR:	I wonder where the others've got to.
EDDIE:	Probably heard you were here, Major.
MAJOR:	Look, here's the Rebel banner Frank Taylor captured at the Waxhaws.
DANIEL:	Ohmigod! Gone right out of my head, ain't none of you heard? How the hell could I forget?
MAJOR:	Heard what?
DANIEL:	It's the drink and thinkin' of Annie.
MAJOR:	Heard what?
DANIEL:	'Bout Frank Taylor! 'Bout Frank!
MAJOR:	What about Frank?
DANIEL:	Shot dead out of his saddle south of town this mornin'.
MAJOR:	Frank Taylor's dead?
DANIEL:	That's what I'm tellin' you, shot out of his saddle—
MAJOR:	What happened?

DANIEL:	Nobody knows. And only one thing sure, it was no stray shot from somebody huntin' off of the road. It was someone he met. Someone who rode right up to him, leavin' just enough space 'tween him and that someone for the barrel of a gun. Boom!
GEORGE:	Who'd want to kill Frank Taylor?
DANIEL:	Damn near everyone who knew him.
MAJOR:	He was as sweet a man as ever you'd meet.
DANIEL:	He was a miserable bastard, and that's not news to anyone here.
MAJOR:	The war changed him.
EDDIE:	He came by it natural.
DANIEL:	The war just shone a light on it.
MAJOR:	Poor Frank.
DANIEL:	Poor be damned. I seen him at Cowan Ford.
MAJOR:	There wasn't a man in the Legion could work a bayonet or a sabre like Frank.
EDDIE:	And I seen him at Waxhaws.
DANIEL:	We ain't talkin' 'bout that.
MAJOR:	It was a bloody one alright and Frank—
DANIEL:	I said I don't want to talk 'bout the battle at Waxhaws!
ANDERSON:	I can understand that.
DANIEL:	No, you can't. You wasn't there, but I know what you heard. Let me tell you somethin'. It was nothin' more than a little white hankie the Rebels tied to a sword. How the hell's a man to see that in the midst of a charge?
ANDERSON:	Were they yellin' for quarter?
DANIEL:	I was followin' Tarleton.
EDDIE:	They got Tarleton's quarter alright.
GEORGE:	What do you mean?
ANDERSON:	Cut down, despite their cries of surrender and absence of arms.
DANIEL:	We ain't here to talk about that!

MAJOR: Benny Tarleton was a bold and brutal man. The times called for that, and I for one was proud to serve him. I'll brook no talk 'gainst Tarleton.

DANIEL: I ain't listenin'!

EDDIE: Well, what we sowed at Waxhaws, we reaped at King's Mountain, Daniel, so it ends up fair all around.

(While the others continue their talk DANIEL bends and bows, quietly singing to himself, to ANNIE, to a stick of wood, improvising a dance and song to his boots.)

DANIEL: *Round and round and round and round look at my boots Annie my boots fine pair of boots look at my boots and love my Annie and love my boots and round and round and these're my boots and closin' my ears and closin' my eyes and lovin' my boots ... (and so on)*

ANDERSON: There was none of the Legion at King's Mountain.

MAJOR: Eddie volunteered, along with our scout, Black Wullie. You should have stuck with the Legion, Eddie.

EDDIE: I admit it. I transferred after Waxhaws thinkin' to escape Bloody Tarleton and I end up at King's Mountain, ain't that a joke?

GEORGE: What's the joke?

EDDIE: Well, there we was, crowded into a little hollow at the top of a hill, surrounded by Rebels, and we was throwin' down our arms and yellin', "Quarter! Quarter!" with Wullie and me havin' a kind of feelin' we'd been there before. And the Rebels, they yell back, "Tarleton's Quarter!"

DANIEL: I ain't listenin'!

EDDIE: And they kept on shootin'.

GEORGE: And?

EDDIE: And?…And we take off our hats, and we sit on our hands and we keep yellin' "Quarter! Quarter!" and the Rebels keep shootin'. And that's it. *(She finds the irony funny.)* We got Tarleton's Quarter alright. Mercy sought. None given.

(With the low sound of the wind, the odd puff of smoke continues to drift from the upstage periphery.)

GEORGE: And?

EDDIE: And what? And after a while they got tired of shootin' so they rounded up what was left of us and hanged six for good measure on the march to prison.

ANDERSON: Yet here you are.

EDDIE: Yeah, well, me and Black Wullie got away one night.

MAJOR: And run straight back to Tarleton's Legion.

EDDIE: Crawled be closer to it, back through the swamps to the Legion, Black Wullie and me.

(A faint, echoing moaning is heard. GEORGE is the only one who hears it.)

MAJOR: And happy enough to be there. For Christ's sake, Wilson! We're not talkin' about Waxhaws. We're talkin' 'bout King's Mountain now!

GEORGE: Did you all come with a horse?

(DANIEL stops singing and dancing.)

DANIEL: No, I walked all the way in these wonderful boots. Of course, I come with a horse!

GEORGE: Did you stable your horse?

MAJOR: Why do you ask?

GEORGE: I just heard a cat out there.

MAJOR: Bloody country.

GEORGE: It's the smell of the pork.

(MAJOR WILLIAMS, DANIEL and GEORGE are collecting their guns and moving off. Smoke drifts past them.)

JOAN: Pink porker.

(The sound of a dry rattle returns. EDDIE picks up her gun.)

EDDIE: So you served with the Loyalist Rangers? *(ANDERSON nods "yes.")* Cherry Valley? *(ANDERSON doesn't respond.)* I once knew a boy with the Rangers. After Cherry Valley he rode away home and put a bullet right here. *(touches*

	ANDERSON's temple with the barrel of her gun) Killed himself.
	(She leaves. After a moment ANDERSON starts to follow her.)
ANNIE:	Stay! Why don't you? Rum, guns, old soldiers, a wanderin' horse and a wild cat could be a deadly combination, Major.
ANDERSON:	If you want.
ANNIE:	You don't like the rum?
ANDERSON:	On occasion I do.
ANNIE:	And this is not that occasion? *(An echoing sound of a shot is followed by an echoing second shot.)* Odds are they'll shoot the roast pig, the horse or each other.
JOAN:	*(To ANDERSON. He holds an attraction for her.)* Richard?
	(The sound of the wind blowing grows a little stronger. ANNIE gets herself a rum.)
ANNIE:	I was just wonderin'.... What I wanted to ask was.... What did you say your name was, Major?
ANDERSON:	I didn't.
ANNIE:	But it is—?
ANDERSON:	John, ma'am.
ANNIE:	John.
ANDERSON:	Major John Anderson.
ANNIE:	John Anderson!
JOAN:	*(Indicating one thumb, then the other.)* John! Andre!
ANNIE:	Good Mama!
	(ANNIE laughs and claps her hands together. JOAN joins in. The sound of the wind carries a hint of murmuring voices.)
ANDERSON:	Ma'am?
JOAN:	John Andre! Who carried the plans for Benedict Arnold!
ANNIE:	An exact correspondence in time and space is what,

	John Anderson?
JOAN:	'Fore his capture by Rebels spent the night under my roof in Tarrytown!
ANNIE:	A notable occurrence of events apparently accidental is what, John Anderson?
JOAN:	Andre under the name of
ANNIE:	Coincidental?
JOAN:	Anderson! John Anderson Andre! while actin' for Arnold who led my Rebel son Richard ... Richard led into battle ...
ANNIE:	Hush, Mama.
JOAN:	Richard.
ANNIE:	The fact is, and what my mother is sayin', is your name's the same as the British-born spy who acted for Arnold. That Major John Andre, callin' himself John Anderson, met with Benedict Arnold behind Rebel lines and afterwards stayed overnight at our farm in Tarrytown.
ANDERSON:	Is that a fact?
ANNIE:	The fact is we were not so much behind the Rebel line, as on it, which had a disconcerting habit of movin' while we remained stationary.
ANDERSON:	A difficult position.
ANNIE:	That Major Anderson Mama mentioned—left in the mornin', took the road to the right 'stead of the left, and was seized by the Rebels.
ANDERSON:	Unfortunate.
ANNIE:	An accident of war. He was hanged.
ANDERSON:	Instead of the traitor.
ANNIE:	You mean Arnold?
ANDERSON:	Benedict Arnold.
ANNIE:	Benedict Arnold, the traitor? Surely that depends on your angle of observation, Major. Benedict Arnold was a Loyalist. If he was a traitor, what then would you call the Rebels?
ANDERSON:	He fought with the Rebels, for the Rebels, led the Rebels 'til he betrayed the Rebels.

JOAN: I want to see your face.

(The faint echo of a shot is heard.)

ANNIE: Personally I'm for the cat.

JOAN: You aren't my son Edward.

ANDERSON: No, ma'am.

JOAN: You knew my son Edward.

ANDERSON: I don't recall meetin' him before this evenin', ma'am, nor
           he me, I believe.

JOAN: Let me look at your face.

ANNIE: I notice you've a powerful recollection of some things, and
           none at all for others.

ANDERSON: An accident of war.

ANNIE: Were you shot in the head?

ANDERSON: (Smiles) No.

ANNIE: Major Andre, the only Anderson we knew prior to you,
           concealed the plans for the defense of West Point 'tween
           the sole of his sock and the sole of his foot. Would you
           hide anything there?

ANDERSON: No, ma'am.

ANNIE: No. A fightin' man wouldn't. If detained by the Rebels, be
           you farmer or spy, the first thing they'd steal would be
           your boots.

ANDERSON: A practice not restricted to Rebels, ma'am.

JOAN: Who did you serve with? Tell me!

ANNIE: Shush.

JOAN: There's somethin' about your face.

ANNIE: Pay her no mind. So the Rebels hauled off his boots, and
           what do they see? Why, this bulgin' outgrowth of sock. So
           off with the sock! I imagine they thought 'twas money.
           Poor Major Andre. He was a very charmin' man. I think he
           took quite a likin' to me, wouldn't you say, Mama?

JOAN: (Referring to ANDERSON.) Likin' to him.

ANNIE: So his misfortune was not in takin' the wrong road, for
           whatever reason, but in his naïve choice of the plan's

	concealment. What would you say?
ANDERSON:	Well ma'am, I'd—
ANNIE:	So many ma'ams—you're a charmin' man, too.
ANDERSON:	I think of myself as a reasonable, rational man.
ANNIE:	So what do you say?
ANDERSON:	Till I'm sure I've all the facts, I hesitate to state an opinion. Have I all the facts?
ANNIE:	Actually, Major Andre was a little too charming. Like trifle is a little too sweet. I've never liked trifle. We haven't had trifle since Boston so I suppose something advantageous came out of the war. So there are your facts. So what do you say?
ANDERSON:	I think it would be best to say nothin' except to assure you that I'm nowhere near as sweet as trifle and considerably less charming than Andre.
ANNIE:	Then you may call me Annie.
ANDERSON:	Would your father approve of that?
ANNIE:	My father approves of hardly anything and puts up with almost everything. Call me Annie, and I'll sing you a song.
ANDERSON:	Annie.
ANNIE:	Would you like the song you were playin' when you arrived?
ANDERSON:	What song was that?

(*ANNIE begins to sing and dance and is joined by JOAN who enjoys dancing to the song.*)

ANNIE AND JOAN:

> *There was an old lady lived over the sea*
> *And she was an Island queen*
> *Her daughter lived off in a new countrie*
> *With an ocean of water between*
> *The old lady's pockets were full of gold*
> *But never contented was she*
> *So she called on her daughter to pay a tax*
> *Of three pence a pound on her tea, her tea*
> *Of three pence a pound on her tea*

The tea was conveyed to her daughter's door
All down by the ocean's side
And the bouncin' girl poured out every pound
In the dark and boilin' tide

(**GEORGE** *appears and hears the song.*)

And then she called out to the Island Queen
Oh mother dear quoth she
Your tea you may have when 'tis steeped enough
But never a tax from me, from me
But never a tax—

(**GEORGE** *enters the space.*)

GEORGE: What the hell're you doin', what're you singin', girl? What the hell, my apologies, Major, she's—

ANNIE: Major Anderson doesn't mind, do you, Major?

ANDERSON: You've a lovely voice.

MAJOR: And it's not to be raised in a Rebel ditty!

ANNIE: Didn't you sing that song?

GEORGE: This girl has a way of wrappin' you 'round with words and then she tightens them up 'til your eyes pop out and you're strugglin' just to draw breath.

ANNIE: Didn't you sing that song?

GEORGE: Yes, I sang that song! I sang that song like many a good Loyalist! I sang and sang 'til I realized our troubles had nothin' to do with the principles of taxation and everything to do with a treacherous movement for separation and independence! There! Are you satisfied!

(**EDDIE** *can be seen on the periphery. She lifts her gun and sights.* **DANIEL**, *unseen by* **EDDIE**, *approaches. He looks to see what she's aiming at.*)

ANNIE: So it's not necessarily a Rebel ditty. What would you say, Major Anderson?

ANDERSON: I'd say it depends on your angle of observation, ma'am.

(*As* **EDDIE** *fires,* **DANIEL** *shoves the barrel of the gun up in*

36   SHARON POLLOCK

the air. The sound of the shot resonates, echoes, then fades away. **THE MAJOR** *yells from off stage.)*

MAJOR: Hey!

DANIEL: What the hell're you doin'?

GEORGE: What's that?

DANIEL: You were shootin' at the Major.

MAJOR: Hey there!

DANIEL: All clear, sir! All clear!

GEORGE: What's goin' on?

DANIEL: Jesus Christ, Eddie.

EDDIE: What's wrong?

DANIEL: You were about to part the Major's hair there and you're askin' me what's wrong?

(THE MAJOR enters.)

EDDIE: I got on my old Legion green and my gun in my hand, and damned if I don't think I see me a traitor. So a crack of the gun and a nice bit of leaf just driftin' down on his head.

DANIEL: You could have killed him.

EDDIE: If I'd really been aimin' at the Major there, I'd've hit the Major 'cause I've a fine eye with a gun. Ain't that right, sir?

MAJOR: Right enough.

GEORGE: No harm done, that's the main thing, eh?

DANIEL: If I hadn't—

GEORGE: A joke, Mr. Wilson. Eh Major? No harm done.

DANIEL: Well then—that's—some sense of humour there. (laughs) Going to rain, eh, going to rain greenery on you while you was just pullin' at a bit of that pig cracklin' and it's a wonderful firepit you got there, Mr. Roberts, and I'm going to build me one just like it, you move me to diggin', I'm inspired to dig—and to eat—and to drink—'cause I says them that ain't here ain't comin' here!!

(More rum is poured; the bread, cheese and sausage are served by **ANNIE** *and* **JOAN**. *Sometime during the following*

they light two lamps which they get from the wagon. They are silent observers of the men. **ANDERSON** *is watchful, cautious.)*

MAJOR:	McMillan never missed a Legion gatherin' yet.
DANIEL:	But he always come with Frank and there ain't no use waitin' for Frank, eh Eddie? Boom! Rode right up to him, somebody did—you know for a moment there, when I seen you under the trees, I thought of Frank.
ANDERSON:	Did you?
DANIEL:	Didn't you notice? So I just laid my gun 'cross the saddle, rested it there like that. Had it in hand, in case, you know.
ANDERSON:	I noticed.
DANIEL:	Do you think McMillan could have done that to Frank?
MAJOR:	Never.
EDDIE:	Frank was one of the Fifty-five.
DANIEL:	That's right.
GEORGE:	What's that got to do with killin' a man?
EDDIE:	Maybe nothin'. Maybe somethin'.
DANIEL:	Eddie's right. Frank was one of the Fifty-five and Frank got his full land allotment as promised while the rest of us is practically squattin', no registration, no nothin'.
EDDIE:	And the most part of Frank's land seized from a soldier's widow.
MAJOR:	Who had not registered the land properly.
EDDIE:	Say some.
DANIEL:	Well how come she couldn't register right and Frank could? That's the question.
EDDIE:	There's some find it easy and there's some find nothin' but blocks thrown in their way by the very ones supposed to be helpin'.
GEORGE:	That's enough.
DANIEL:	He's right.
MAJOR:	You know no more of the problem than a fish knows of flyin'.

EDDIE:	We know one thing! We know the agents directed to act in the interests of all are actin' on behalf of the Fifty-five and we know you're one of them!
MAJOR:	What the hell did we fight for if not the preservation of worth and class that's the very foundation of Empire?
ANDERSON:	*(To EDDIE)* What did you fight for?
GEORGE:	Eddie fought for King and Country knowin' the English Parliament's treatment of us was an act of human frailty.
MAJOR:	That could be corrected in time by good men workin' within ordered and proper procedures.
GEORGE:	If worst came to worst preferrin' one tyrant three thousand miles away to three thousand tyrants one mile away.
MAJOR:	The rule of the mob.
EDDIE:	The people.
MAJOR:	You talk like a Rebel.
EDDIE:	I speak of the betrayin' of what we was promised and you call me a Rebel? Me who's killed Rebels from Waxhaws to Camden, King's Mountain to Yorkton!
MAJOR:	What you speak is sedition and treason and best forgot by all of us here.
EDDIE:	Is any opposition rebellion?
GEORGE:	It's not the time for questionin'! It's time for restorin' order and rank and stability. It's time to get on with our lives.
EDDIE:	So our promised land, our great new province, this country will become the fiefdom of a few, is that it?
GEORGE:	Our position—
EDDIE:	Former position—
GEORGE:	—gives us rights, can't you see that?
EDDIE:	It's not what I'm lookin' at.
MAJOR:	Had your father been in New York when the Committee of Fifty-five Families was formed, why of course his name as a foremost citizen of Boston'd be there with the rest.

GEORGE: You hear that, Eddie? So we benefit from the state of things. It's just a matter of declarin', publicly declarin' so to speak, for the Fifty-five.

EDDIE: And for the election of their slate for Assembly.

GEORGE: You see? Eddie listens.

MAJOR: And that which I mentioned before, about the alternate candidates and their strategies, that information too should be forthcomin' from you, Eddie.

EDDIE: And Daniel here, what's in it for him?

DANIEL: I got no position but I sure as hell would like to get my plot registered.

EDDIE: And if they decide to come and throw you off like the widow woman and give it to someone who stands higher with the Fifty-five, what then?

DANIEL: Jesus, Eddie—I—I've trusted the Major here with my life on occasion, I guess I'd just have to trust him with my land registration.

GEORGE: You see, Eddie?

EDDIE: And what about them that aren't here tonight, what about their land registration?

DANIEL: I dunno, Eddie! I got enough trouble lookin' after myself, what else do you want me to do?

GEORGE: That sense of justice and fair play, that's a good thing, but it's got to be tempered with a sense of reality, Eddie. You'll learn.

EDDIE: You don't know who I am or what I think.

GEORGE: 'Course I do.

EDDIE: You think you do but you don't.

GEORGE: What kind of crazy talk is that?

EDDIE: Let's talk about smashin' a man's skull with the butt of my gun, and wipin' his brains off of my sleeve. Or leanin' down from my horse and slicin' a man who's run out of powder, knowin' to stay my arm can mean my own death or the death of my friends. Let's talk about sightin' down the barrel of my gun and seein' the face of a neighbour,

	knowin' I might see the face of my brother sightin' down the barrel of his gun at me! And for what? That's what's crazy!
GEORGE:	No more, no more!
MAJOR:	There's some things have to be done and we had to do them.
EDDIE:	To stop and think then was to die, but now? Now I ask, what did we do it for?
MAJOR:	Loyalty to our country, trust in Parliament and the King.
EDDIE:	Are they to be trusted?
GEORGE:	Eddie—
EDDIE:	You know nothin' about it and you know nothin' 'bout me!
GEORGE:	I'm your father, I know you better than anyone! You sit down, sit down! The rum's gone to your head.

(Several quick flashes of lightning are followed by a roll of thunder, which echoes and fades. A faint dry rattle is heard.)

DANIEL:	We're not here to argue and fight, we're here to remember. Where's your green, Major, the Legion jacket that took you to war? I'm wearin' mine, and Eddie's got his, where the hell's yours?

(He tosses a green jacket to THE MAJOR.)

There you go Major.

MAJOR:	*(As he struggles into his green jacket.)* The damn thing has shrunk.
DANIEL:	Or your belly has grown, eh Eddie? Come on Eddie! Ta-dum! Ta-dum! There you go, Major, this one should fit, ta-dum!

(THE MAJOR puts down the green jacket. DANIEL throws the iron helmet and the uniform jacket with the lace epaulettes to THE MAJOR. He will wear both although they do not fit.)

Ta-dum! A toast! A toast! Rum all around! There may be just a few of us here, but we're still rememberin'—that's what we're here for. What else are we here for, Major?

(GEORGE *puts up a large picture of Tarleton pulling on his boots.*)

DANIEL: (*A toast*) Here's to Tarleton's Legion!

MAJOR: Here's to them that served and fell! Here's to them who can't be with us!

DANIEL: And may the Rebels burn in Hell!

(DANIEL *pounds on a drum and the others, with the exception of* ANDERSON, JOAN *and* ANNIE, *drink the toast. They are moving into the formal ritual of their Remembrance Ceremony, taking up positions, ready for speeches. The sense of occasion is undercut every once in a while by a comment or reaction not appropriate to the ceremony.* DANIEL *sings solemnly, as he would a hymn; it's the song that the Loyalists sang in defiance as they surrendered to the Rebels at Yorktown, the battle that marked England's defeat.*)

DANIEL: *If buttercups buzzed after the bee*
If boats were on land

(THE MAJOR *joins in.*)

Churches on sea

(GEORGE *joins in.*)

If ponies rode men and grass ate the cow
If cats should be chased into holes by the mice
And mamas sold babies for just half a crown
If spring were summer and the other way round
Then all of the world would be upside down!

EDDIE: And not such a bad thing if it were.

GEORGE: (*Clears his throat; it's the first time he's participated in the Remembering.*) May I say somethin'?... I want to say somethin'. I may not have had the honour of servin' with Tarleton, but I admire and envy you all. With two of my—

With Eddie away, my job was to see to the women, my
good woman and Annie. As to the Rememberin', I can't
share that with you, much as I'd like to, but joinin' you
tonight, I'm going to take the liberty of donnin' my one
and only trophy of war—and this, sirs, is it.

(GEORGE holds up the blood-stained waistcoat.)

ANDERSON: Where did you get it?

GEORGE: *(As he struggles into it.)* Well sir, when the Rebels fled
Bunker Hill—gimme a hand, Abijah—with the English
hot on their heels, a few loyal citizens like myself were
there for what help we could give—I'll just leave it
open—and we were checkin' the Rebel fallen—

EDDIE: Were you?

GEORGE: What?

EDDIE: Checkin' the Rebel fallen?

GEORGE: I just said I was.

EDDIE: Were you lookin' for Richard?

GEORGE: I was not lookin' for anyone! Listen to what I say! I say
me and a few others were checkin' the fallen and I come
on this figure lyin' face down in the mud ... a young
man, with a blue waistcoat and a blond head of hair.
He'd been leading the Rebel charge and now, now he lay
in the mud ... I remember ... remember his hair—
looking tidy and combed, in the mud ... and I ...
*(ANDERSON takes a drink of his rum. GEORGE, in the
telling, has begun to feel a sense of shame.)* And I ... took
the man's waistcoat ... this is his waistcoat ... the
waistcoat of one of the Rebel fallen ... at Bunker Hill.

ANDERSON: *(Referring to what THE MAJOR has donned.)* And that is
the helmet of Baron de Kalb who led the Rebel forces at
Camden—and that is his jacket with the lace epaulettes
that he wore at the battle of Camden.

MAJOR: Where almost two thousand Rebels flung down their
muskets, turned tail, and run! Huzzaaaa!

ANDERSON: De Kalb and the Delaware Continentals didn't run.

MAJOR:	True enough.
ANDERSON:	Five hundred Rebels against two thousand Royalists! De Kalb and the Continentals stood firm. But when Tarleton's Legion charged, de Kalb went down. He was dyin' and one of you hauled him up, propped him 'gainst a wagon, and twisted him out of his coat! And he stood there, clingin' to the wagon while the blood poured through his shirt and his breeches. Which one of you boys was it?
DANIEL:	*(Uneasy)* We're talkin' 'bout Yorktown.
EDDIE:	I don't recall your outfit the Loyalist Rangers bein' at Camden.
MAJOR:	I know goddamn well they weren't.
DANIEL:	To hell with Camden! Did you serve at Yorktown?
ANDERSON:	I was there.
DANIEL:	Well we're Rememberin' Yorktown! Now! *(Back to the ceremony.)* I can see that place on the inside of my eyeballs. I can hear it in my ears. The band playin' sweet and pure, "If buttercups buzzed after the bee ..." And then the silence. I can hear the quiet with us marchin' out to the surrender ground ...
MAJOR:	'Tween two lines of Rebels.
DANIEL:	I seen George Washington there on a big bay horse. You seen him too, Eddie.
EDDIE:	*(To ANDERSON)* So were you at Camden or not?
DANIEL:	I thought we was Rememberin' the Surrender at Yorktown!
MAJOR:	We are!
DANIEL:	Alright then! *(He gives a roll on the drum.)* We was wearin' our Tarleton Loyalist Legion Green, and the Rebels, they had hardly no uniforms at all, they was wearin' old huntin' shirts, or a kind of brown shirt—
EDDIE:	*(Low to ANDERSON.)* What were you wearin'?
MAJOR:	The English in red, scarlet red—
DANIEL:	Was like wearin' a bullseye tied to your chest in the woods.
MAJOR:	They was never meant to fight in the woods! Proper battle fields was what they were meant for!

DANIEL:	And our Hessian allies? Four foot of hat, boots up to their arse, big bloody sword hangin' down catchin' in the bush every step they took, no wonder we lost the war!
MAJOR:	We're Rememberin' Yorktown!
DANIEL:	I'm Rememberin' Yorktown!
MAJOR:	Well you're not Rememberin' right!
EDDIE:	For Christ's sake let's get on with it.
GEORGE:	(Sings lustily trying to get them back on track.) If buttercups buzzed after the bee If boats were on land—
MAJOR:	The Band Playin' Loud and Clear
DANIEL:	(Sings, joining GEORGE) If boats were on land and churches on sea—
MAJOR:	Marchin' out! Layin' down our arms! Men weepin'—
DANIEL:	And little Charlie Meyers who busted his drum rather than give it over to Rebels—no Rebel drummer boy'd beat on his drum—and this here's the drum Charlie was given in New York, the only belongin' the boy had to transport when we sailed to this place—
MAJOR:	The Beat of the Drum! the Scream of the Fifes! And the—
DANIEL:	I want to Remember Charlie Meyers!
MAJOR:	Charlie died after the war.
DANIEL:	I don't give a damn! This is his drum and I want to remember him, eh Eddie?
MAJOR:	Later, Corporal!
DANIEL:	Now, Major! I'm going to remember little Charlie Meyers who died in my arms of—What did he die of, Eddie?
EDDIE:	The cold and the crowdin' and the stinkin' smells of the Exodus ship.
DANIEL:	... who died ... in my arms. He was a good boy and would have been ... an asset! to this god forsaken place ... had he got here!

(Pause)

MAJOR: Are you finished?

DANIEL: I'm finished.

MAJOR: And the Clatter of Grounded Arms!

           (Pause)

DANIEL   Is that it?

MAJOR   That's it.

           (DANIEL gives a roll of the drum, then tosses it to EDDIE who beats it as DANIEL grabs THE MAJOR, singing and dancing with him.)

DANIEL: *Come!*
           'Round the heather
           Come o'er the heather
           (To EDDIE) Play!
           You're welcome late and early
           Around—(to EDDIE) keep playin'!
           Around him fling your royal King

           (DANIEL "flings" THE MAJOR at GEORGE; they dance together as DANIEL grabs ANNIE. The dance becomes faster and faster, more and more frantic, as ALL sing, EDDIE drums. JOAN does her own little dance.)

ALL: *(Singing) For who'll be King but Charlie*
           Charlie likes to kiss the girls
           Charlie likes the brandy
           Charlie likes to kiss the girls
           Whenever they come handy

           (DANIEL kisses ANNIE and they dance, laughing and singing. GEORGE grabs JOAN and the two of them dance and sing. WULLIE, with his gun, enters, and is a shadowy figure on the periphery, watching, coming closer.)

           Charlie likes to hold the girls
           Charlie likes the brandy
           Charlie likes to kiss the girls
           Whenever they come handy ooooohh
           Come 'round the heather

ANNIE:	You and your drum and your dancin', I never met a sillier man, Daniel Wilson!
DANIEL:	I fell in love with you the first time I seen you. Marry me, Annie!
	(As the song and dance continues, THE MAJOR *collapses coughing and laughing.* WULLIE *moves on with his gun.* EDDIE *is the first to notice* WULLIE.*)*
EDDIE:	Wullie? *(She stops drumming, and the singing and dancing stops with everyone close to collapse.)*
WULLIE:	What be happenin' here?
MAJOR:	What's he doin' here?
DANIEL:	Legion get-together, Wullie!
MAJOR:	Anniversary of the Fall of Yorktown. What're you doin' here?
EDDIE:	You'd have had an invite if I knew you was 'round.
WULLIE:	Today be the 22nd.
MAJOR:	That's right.
WULLIE:	You be three days out.
EDDIE:	Annie, how about a rum for Wullie?
MAJOR:	What're you sayin'!
WULLIE :	Fall of Yorktown be October 19th.
MAJOR:	October 22nd!
WULLIE :	No sir, 19th.
DANIEL:	*(Laughs)* I think he's right.
MAJOR:	So what're you here for then if you think the Rememberin' should be the 19th and this here's the 22nd?
WULLIE:	Ole Frank be here?
DANIEL:	Frank's dead, Wullie.
WULLIE:	Dead? That true, Eddie?
EDDIE:	True enough. He took a ball through the chest south of town this mornin'.
WULLIE:	Frank Taylor's dead.
DANIEL:	You look like hell, what've you been doin'?

MAJOR:	I said, if you ain't here for the Gatherin', why're you here?
EDDIE:	Can't a man visit a friend?
MAJOR:	Wullie?
EDDIE:	He don't answer to you. How's Shelbourne, Wullie?
MAJOR:	Wullie!
EDDIE:	Keep your mouth shut 'til he's welcomed proper! This here's a man who's closer to me than any man, and by God, Wullie, it's good to see you.
WULLIE:	Frank's dead?
EDDIE:	That's right.
DANIEL:	Jesus, man, you're skinny, ain't they got no eats in Shelbourne?
WULLIE:	Coloureds done be run out of Shelbourne, we over in Birchtown now. People sold everything, now they starvin' and sellin' themselves back into bondage.
EDDIE:	What about your land allotment and rations?
WULLIE:	Molasses and meal, and that give out after White rations. Most often, nothin' left.
EDDIE:	And the land?
WULLIE:	We can't get title.
EDDIE:	Again the King's gratitude to Loyalists, eh Major?
WULLIE:	*(Starting to laugh)* Frank Taylor's dead, right, Eddie? *(He puts down his gun.)* He's dead and here I be, walkin' on my feet, crawlin' on my belly all the way from Birchtown to here, and you tell me Frank Taylor's dead? I come all this way to get you to read this and help me—*(he takes a document from his pocket and gives it to* **EDDIE**)—and Frank Taylor's dead!
MAJOR:	It don't call for laughin', boy.
	*(**WULLIE** notices **ANDERSON**.)*
DANIEL:	What's it say?
EDDIE:	It's an indenture agreement ... 'tween Wullie and Frank ... back into bondage—for thirty-nine years? Wullie?

WULLIE:	*(His attention is pulled back to EDDIE.)* Yeah? Is that it? Well that ole Frank tole me one year. One year 'stead of thirty-nine—but it don't matter now, eh Eddie?
MAJOR:	Frank's got heirs, ain't he?
EDDIE:	What'd you sign this for?
WULLIE:	Well I'll tell you, ole Frank come to Birchtown and he tells me I ain't no freed slave.
EDDIE:	You got your certificate, did you show him that?
WULLIE:	Frank say he's going to swear he heard you and me Eddie, us talkin' 'bout how I couldn't get no certificate 'cause I can't prove I run away from a Rebel. Frank say this certificate be false, be forged, got your writin' on it and be no good. He swears he heard us talkin' 'bout doin' that and he say he need a big black man like me. If I make my mark, one year service, he won't say nothin' ... We starvin' and freezin' in Birchtown, so I ... I make my mark.
MAJOR:	You're in trouble.
WULLIE:	After, I looks at the paper and I looks at the paper, and I gets to thinkin' 'bout Frank and I gets scared. Thirty-nine years you say? When he tells me one? Ain't that just like ole Frank?
	(EDDIE burns the document in the flame of one of the lamps.)
MAJOR:	You think that's the end of it? He's property. He goes with the goods and the rest of the real estate.
	(ANDERSON will make a slow, subtle move towards his gun and pick it up.)
WULLIE:	But I has my certificate sayin' I'm free!
MAJOR:	Eddie forged it. You just told us that.
WULLIE:	The certificate's good, ain't it, Eddie?
EDDIE:	It's good.
DANIEL:	Well that don't make no difference, the Major says you be Frank's property now, burnt up indenture paper or not.
MAJOR:	Where was you this mornin'?

WULLIE:	Me, I be—
MAJOR:	Was you south of town? (*WULLIE makes a move for his gun.*) Take him!

(*DANIEL, THE MAJOR, and GEORGE seize WULLIE, who resists. They wrestle him to the floor with difficulty. EDDIE tries to assist WULLIE. ANNIE and JOAN watch. Just as WULLIE is subdued, ANDERSON fires a shot in the air from his long gun. He pulls the flag from the table. The faint sound of the band playing* The Day the World Turned Upside Down *fades in. ANDERSON stands with the flag draped over one shoulder, his gun covering the others. The light is falling as the music rises.*)

ANDERSON: Gentlemen!

(*The men and women look to him as he stands with the gun aimed at them. The sound of the band increases.*)

Blackout

END OF ACT ONE

ACT TWO

∾

> (*The Day the World Turned Upside Down is fading as*
> *light comes up on the scene as seen at the end of Act One*)

ANDERSON: Gentlemen!

DANIEL: You could have just given a whoop!

MAJOR: No need for weaponry, friend.

GEORGE: No sir, he's collared.

> (**ANDERSON** *makes a motion with the gun, and they drag*
> **WULLIE** *to his feet and shove him in that direction.* **EDDIE**
> *grabs* **WULLIE** *and pulls him back. A look exchanged*
> *between the two of them.* **WULLIE** *starts to slide a knife*
> *surreptitiously out.* **ANDERSON** *motions for them all to*
> *move in one direction.*)

ANDERSON: All of you!

DANIEL: Eh?

MAJOR: All?

ANDERSON: All of you! (*They move together.*) Wullie. The knife, on the floor.

> (**WULLIE** *slides his knife across the floor to* **ANDERSON**.
> **EDDIE** *is inching towards* **ANDERSON**)

MAJOR: But it's the black killed Frank!

GEORGE: Don't worry, it'll all be legal and proper.

MAJOR: It's alright, we're goin' to take him into town and hang him.

DANIEL: Somethin's wrong here.

> (**ANDERSON** *draws a pistol from his jacket.*)

GEORGE: We can't allow you to take him! He's gotta go into town.

MAJOR: He'll get justice on Friday. I give you my word.

(EDDIE steps towards ANDERSON who points the pistol directly at EDDIE.)

ANDERSON: No further.

DANIEL: What t'hell's goin' on?

(EDDIE backs off.)

WULLIE: I know the man's face.

DANIEL: You mean him? *(ANDERSON)*

WULLIE: Him ... when I was scoutin' ... one time I gets picked up by Rebels and this ... be one of them Rebels.

ANDERSON: And you played the Patriot Buck and we let you go.

WULLIE: He be with de Kalb and the Continentals then.

MAJOR: Washington's Delaware Continentals!

GEORGE: A goddamn Rebel!

ANDERSON: Patriot, sir.

MAJOR: Why the hell didn't you name him?

(He hits WULLIE. EDDIE shoves THE MAJOR knocking him down.)

GEORGE: No Eddie.

ANDERSON: Easy! Does none of you wonder why a Patriot Son of Liberty would share a meal and memories with tea drinkers and traitors?

GEORGE: Who be the traitor here?

ANDERSON: And who be the King's lap dog?

MAJOR: What were the Sons of Liberty but a terrorist gang bent on stealin' and tarrin' and featherin'!

ANDERSON: And you're the ones spoke 'gainst tyranny, but when it came time to stand bold 'gainst a tyrant, there was no man amongst you!

(GEORGE spits at ANDERSON who points the gun at him and he retreats.)

DANIEL: What do you want?

ANDERSON: Justice.

MAJOR:	You want Wullie?
WULLIE:	I didn't kill no one!
ANDERSON:	Then you were one hell of a poor soldier, Wullie.
EDDIE:	You take Wullie, you take me first.
ANDERSON:	I may want you first.
DANIEL:	So what do you want?
ANDERSON:	I had a brother.
DANIEL:	We never heard of you so how the hell could we know your brother!
ANDERSON:	My brother was murdered as Waxhaws. Cut to pieces with the rest of them that surrendered.
MAJOR:	Nobody was murdered at Waxhaws! That was an act of war and men fell in battle!
ANDERSON:	The slaughter of surrendered men is murder.
GEORGE:	Do you know some court of law where some soldier's been charged with that by his peers?
MAJOR:	And convicted?
ANDERSON:	*(Laughs)* You Loyalists got a habit of confusin' legality and justice.
EDDIE:	What about King's Mountain?
ANDERSON:	What about it?
EDDIE:	Rebels killed Loyalists there. We called quarter and surrendered and they killed us, we threw down our guns and they killed us, we sat on the ground—
WULLIE:	And we sat on our hands—
EDDIE:	And they killed us.
GEORGE:	You don't call that some kind of justice?
ANDERSON:	I call it murder on murder, like the boots of a corpse makin' its rounds.
MAJOR:	So you had a brother, so he died at Waxhaws.
ANDERSON:	Do none of you understand? The sentence for murder is death. I intend executin' the one of you here, or any one of you here, before I leave tonight.

DANIEL:	Are you crazy?
ANDERSON:	What do you think?

(DANIEL slowly approaches ANDERSON as he speaks)

DANIEL:	I think you're crazier than hell! You weren't at the Waxhaws, you don't know what the hell happened there! I told you, the Rebels sent a fella out with a little white hankie tied to the tip of a sword. Who the hell could see that? And right then, at the same time, Tarleton's horse went down, ain't that right? And Tarleton under it! We all thought he was dead and we—you're a fightin' man, you must know—it ... it was like a slaughter pen, and a sabre goes through flesh like a hot knife through butter and no one gave the order to stop and ... and ... ain't none of us proud of what happened that day—

(DANIEL goes to grab ANDERSON. ANDERSON kicks out at him, getting him in the mouth, knocking him down.)

ANDERSON:	But when it was over, well over, some of you went from one pile of bodies to another, pullin' off the dead and killin' the wounded and livin'. And one of the livin' was a fourteen-year-old boy who had time to cry "quarter" 'fore the sabre came down. Do you remember that boy? ... None of you remembers that boy?
DANIEL:	We don't want to remember. We spend time forgettin'.
ANDERSON:	Well I can't forget, nor do I want to.
EDDIE:	Or forgive?
MAJOR:	There's nothin' to forgive!
GEORGE:	What about justice for them that was stoned and hanged and died of a tarrin' for remainin' Loyal!
ANDERSON:	And look what you got for it. Eddie can't even register land.
MAJOR:	So in the name of justice you come to commit murder on one of us here—well, choose your scapegoat and go!
DANIEL:	Hold on.
MAJOR:	The province is peopled with soldiers, and once you leave here, you'll not make the border. So choose!

ANDERSON: You choose.

DANIEL: One of us?

ANDERSON: Or let the responsible one step forward. Was it you?

WULLIE: Not Eddie.

EDDIE: Shut up, Wullie.

DANIEL: Why're you so certain it's one of us here?

ANDERSON: A witness.

MAJOR: Who?

DANIEL: It weren't none of us here!

ANDERSON: There's always a witness. Could be one who escaped in the woods. One who didn't beg quarter and lived. Could be one of your own who'd try to barter the name for his life. So—step forward—or choose.

MAJOR: We—are not going to choose.

ANDERSON: I choose then. I choose ... you, ma'am. (*He is referring to* ANNIE.)

GEORGE: No!

DANIEL: You can't do that!

ANDERSON: An innocent, which is fitting and proper. Historically accurate.

> (ANDERSON *carefully leans his long gun on a wagon shaft or barrel close at hand.*)

GEORGE: No.

ANDERSON: I thought royalty lovers would appreciate that.

EDDIE: Don't talk about royalty, talk about the rightness of now, this action right now.

ANDERSON: Responsibility denied for the death of my brother, denied again by refusin' to choose. Who always pays when them that can, don't? The innocent pay. Step forward, ma'am.

DANIEL: Annie had nothin' to do with it!

ANDERSON: She pays for your refusal to act. You choose this by refusin' to choose.

GEORGE: Wait.

DANIEL: Kill me 'stead of Annie!

ANDERSON: That wouldn't be justice 'less you be the one.

GEORGE: What is it you want?

ANDERSON: Responsibility acknowledged, and twice you refuse.

EDDIE: Even St. Peter got three cracks at denyin'. Ask the question again.

ANDERSON: Let the responsible one step forward.

(*No one moves. He shoves* ANNIE, *she falls down. He aims the pistol at her head.*)

MAJOR: We'll choose.

(DANIEL, GEORGE, THE MAJOR, WULLIE *and* EDDIE *move away to consult while Joan approaches* ANDERSON *slowly, tentatively.* ANNIE *is still down.*)

JOAN: Lost. I lost my oldest. Richard, my oldest? Can that which is lost be found? Lost Edward my youngest, and Richard, he was just standin' there at the end of the walk and he raised his hand in a bit of a wave and then he was gone. And the walk?

MAJOR: (*Low*) Any of you got a pistol?

DANIEL: Got a knife.

JOAN: The walk? The walk it was empty, and Edward? Edward lay on the bed and he stared at the ceilin'. And Em'ly? There was seven minutes between them and I'd sit in the parlour, it was a wonderful room with ... and ... over there, and here ... (*To* ANDERSON) and, do you remember that?

ANNIE: Hush, Mama.

JOAN: (*To* ANDERSON) You can whisper.

MAJOR: You're good with a knife, eh Wullie, at throwin' a knife?

EDDIE: There's no way of takin' him 'less he fires at least the pistol.

DANIEL: And the person who'd take that ball is Annie. You said we'd choose and I say we do that.

GEORGE: Is he right? 'Bout one of you at the Waxhaws?

JOAN:	Annie would sit in the rocker with both of them, arm round each of 'em, Edward and Em'ly, and Richard would rock 'em, stand behind them and push and the rocker would rock and Richard would sing sweet and clear, clear and sweet.

(Sings)

Hi says the little leather winged bat
I will tell you the reason that

(A child's voice joins JOAN's. It is very faint and can hardly be heard.)

The reason that I cry in the night
Is because I lost my heart's delight
Hi says the little mourning dove

(JOAN stops singing but the child's voice continues for a moment.)

I'll tell you how to win her love

ANNIE:	It's alright, Mama, shush.
JOAN:	*(Whispers to ANDERSON)* Do you know that song?

(The light is now fully on the men and EDDIE.)

GEORGE:	I mean, if one of you at the Waxhaws did that, I mean, don't that bear on the matter if one of you—
MAJOR:	No.
GEORGE:	No?
MAJOR:	That's his path, not ours.
GEORGE:	But if the guilty one's here, why—
DANIEL:	If that person don't choose to step forward then that person don't step forward. Ain't nobody going to point their finger at nobody.
MAJOR:	We all be guilty and we all be innocent. We were followin' orders and responsibility and murder don't come into it!
DANIEL:	You was givin' quite a few of those orders back then.
MAJOR:	They came to me, I passed them onto you.

DANIEL:	I don't suppose we can choose Tarleton if he ain't here.
MAJOR:	Tarleton was followin' orders, it's a war, for Christ's sake!
EDDIE:	Nothin' goes up the ladder, it always comes down.
GEORGE:	But surely if one of you—
MAJOR:	I said no!
EDDIE:	I'll step forward.
GEORGE:	But you're not the one, Eddie, are you?
DANIEL:	Get some straws and we'll draw on it.
MAJOR:	Goddamn it, you don't order a man to his death on the length of a straw, is that civilized?
GEORGE:	I wasn't there.
DANIEL:	He wasn't there.
EDDIE:	So this civilized process of "all is innocent and all is guilty" only applies to them that was actually there?
MAJOR:	Well, I dunno, I—
EDDIE:	Eh?
MAJOR:	I'm thinkin'! … Right! Citizen and soldier, all both innocent and guilty in war.
EDDIE:	And Annie?
MAJOR:	Not women!
DANIEL:	Women don't come into it!
MAJOR:	But the rest of us, we all share in the Waxhaws.
EDDIE:	Equally?
MAJOR:	Keep your mouth shut, Eddie, and listen! If we don't do this properly we're no better than the Rebel. The group chooses, agreed?
DANIEL:	Agreed.
GEORGE:	Agreed.
MAJOR:	Agreed. We choose one and that one sacrifices all for the others and Annie. And that one'll die knowin' the Rebel will hang for it. If we have to drag him tied to a horse out of Delaware, we'll do it.
DANIEL:	Agreed.
GEORGE:	Agreed.

WULLIE: What if I be chose?

DANIEL: What if he be chose? Ain't never been a White man hanged for killin' a Coloured.

WULLIE: If I get chose, I'll sorely miss seein' that hangin'. I'd wager that'll be a hangin' you'll all miss seein'. Ain't nobody going to see that event.

DANIEL: Wullie's right.

MAJOR: If Wullie be chose … we take the Rebel's money … and assets worth Wullie's thirty-nine years of indentured service to Frank … and give it to Frank's heirs! Fair and legal, ain't that the law?

DANIEL: It's the law alright.

MAJOR: That's right. But there's somethin' else I'm thinkin'—any of us could be chose 'cause we all share in the Waxhaws …

DANIEL: Yeah?

MAJOR: But— *(He considers* WULLIE.*)* We don't all share in the killin' of Frank. That was no act of war, that was murder, pure and simple!

> *(Lights change. The focus is now on* ANNIE, ANDERSON *and* JOAN, *who hums softly as she rocks back and forth.)*

ANNIE: *(Getting up)* Could you kill me lookin' me right in the face?

ANDERSON: If I had to.

JOAN: Do you believe a lion can lie down with a lamb?

ANDERSON: I can see the two of them lyin' down alright, but I can see only one of them gettin' up.

JOAN: *(Laughs)* No no no no no.

ANNIE: My brother believed a lion could lie down with a lamb, and both of 'em get up again.

ANDERSON: Eddie?

JOAN: Not Eddie, no.

ANNIE: Richard, the oldest. It was impossible for Richard to sit down at table with Father without havin' words, ugly words, and yet Richard believed lions could lie down with lambs and he saw no contradiction in that. He fought with Arnold at Quebec. He died at Saratoga. Least that's what we heard.

JOAN:	No no no.
ANDERSON:	A patriot?
ANNIE:	Richard. I saw him once in the prison ship. You don't believe me? I did. I made my way there. I offered somethin'. Them in charge wanted it. I gave it to them. It meant nothin' to me. You could have it too if you want ... Afterwards, they let me see him ... and after that, I gave it to them again. Or they took it. When I saw him, my brother, he told me the worst fightin' he'd seen was 'tween two prisoners over a rat. He laughed.
ANDERSON:	Why tell me?
ANNIE:	After he was exchanged he fought under Arnold at Saratoga. We heard that's where he died.
ANDERSON:	Do you think you can bargain with that?
ANNIE:	He looked so thin.

(Lights are changing to focus on THE MAJOR and the men.)

ANDERSON:	*(Steps away from the women)* You can't bargain with that.
JOAN:	Bargain with that!
ANDERSON:	You have 'til dawn!
MAJOR:	Alright!
DANIEL:	I thought the Rebels killed Frank.
GEORGE:	I thought you thought Wullie did.
DANIEL:	That was before the Rebel said Frank was his witness.
GEORGE:	Did he say that?
MAJOR:	He was playin' with us, gettin' us goin'.
DANIEL:	Well he was going to kill me if I hadn't the gun right there on the saddle.
MAJOR:	The Rebel wants the responsible one—or an innocent one—or the one that we choose—so why would the Rebel kill Frank?
DANIEL:	He'd do it to get on to us!
MAJOR:	But Wullie here—
WULLIE:	Didn't do nothin' to Frank!

MAJOR:	He shot him to get out of indentured service!
WULLIE:	Then why'd I come to see Eddie?
MAJOR:	To tell him Frank knew 'bout the certificate Eddie forged sayin' you be a freed runaway Rebel slave.
EDDIE:	The certificate's good.
WULLIE:	I come to get Eddie to read my indenture paper cause Frank tells me one year service, but I don't trust him. I make my mark thinkin' one year!
MAJOR:	Who says?
WULLIE:	I do!
MAJOR:	Unsubstantiated! You got a White man's word for that?
WULLIE:	I had to take a White man's word 'cause I can't read!
MAJOR:	You must have some old darkie 'round can read, tell you thirty-nine years 'stead of one.
WULLIE:	I come to Eddie to read it!
DANIEL:	If Wullie don't know it's thirty-nine years, why'd he kill Frank?
MAJOR:	Wullie knew!
DANIEL:	He says—
MAJOR:	Frank told Wullie thirty-nine years when he signed!
WULLIE:	No!
MAJOR:	Told him 'fore he signed.
DANIEL:	Wullie says no.
MAJOR:	Unsubstantiated! So if Wullie be guilty of the murder of Frank, and we so find him, I say let Wullie be the one we choose for the Rebel!
EDDIE:	I could have killed Frank. I was out all day and Frank was a man I wouldn't mind killin'.
GEORGE:	Keep your mouth shut.
MAJOR:	We'll vote on it.
EDDIE:	Who votes?
MAJOR:	All of us here.
EDDIE:	Includin' Wullie?

MAJOR:	The accused don't vote!
EDDIE:	What're you? Judge? Prosecutor? I don't think you can vote. Not if we want it done proper.
MAJOR:	Well—
EDDIE:	I can't vote. I'm confessin' to the murder of Frank Taylor.
MAJOR:	You can't do that!
EDDIE:	That leaves Daniel—and you, father.
DANIEL:	The Rebel killed Frank! You wasn't with me when I seen him under the trees. The hair came up on the back of my neck, was like seein' a ghost, and then he give his horse a bit of a nudge, and when he got clear of the trees, he was just another man like myself. A soldierin' man. I could tell. One of us. That's what I thought.
MAJOR:	You brought a viper into the nest, Corporal.
DANIEL:	Well it's a bit late for that now. All I know is here's Eddie sayin' he killed Frank, and you sayin' Wullie killed Frank, and me thinkin' the Rebel killed Frank, and one of us is going to get killed and none of this is gettin' us any further ahead!
MAJOR:	You don't choose a man for death without some kind of due process and I'm doin' my best to find one!
EDDIE:	Perhaps there's no such thing.
MAJOR:	You got no respect for position or placement! There's the reason we lost the war!
DANIEL:	If we can't volunteer and we're not drawin' straws, nor pressgangin' Wullie, what the hell are we doin'?
	(Pause)
GEORGE:	Would it be right to say ... that some ... not just us here now, but at large, some are more valuable to the community and all ... do you understand what I'm sayin'?
WULLIE:	This one understands—it's the kind of thing a Coloured man don't have no trouble at all understandin'.
GEORGE:	Such things are generally understood. You can't have people without you have some kind of relationship

between people, some kind of rankin', some kind of value put on their contribution and placement.

MAJOR: Go on.

GEORGE: Does it make some kind of sense that the least valuable to the community be the one that we choose, if choose we must?

MAJOR: All to be done equal and democratic.

DANIEL: How can that be done with Wullie here?

EDDIE: *(Low)* Gimme that knife, Daniel.

DANIEL: What for?

EDDIE: Just give it.

(DANIEL *slips the knife to* EDDIE)

MAJOR: We each of us, Wullie too, makes our case and we assess all of the cases and we vote, each gettin' a vote, agreed?

EDDIE: I want you to know that if I get any sense at all, the littlest feeling that things ain't runnin' democratic and equal

(DANIEL *stands as to obscure* ANDERSON'S *vision as* EDDIE *grabs* THE MAJOR *and places the knife against his throat.*)

I'm going to cut your throat. I'm going to kill you dead as I killed Frank.

DANIEL: You never did, Eddie.

EDDIE: Either I did, or the Rebel did, take your pick.

MAJOR: Equal and democratic, I swear it, we each state our case and we vote on it.

(EDDIE *releases* THE MAJOR. *Morning light grows on* ANDERSON, ANNIE *and* JOAN.)

JOAN: My mother ... my mother spoke of a soft rain. She'd visit the grave of my father with a soft rain fallin'. No soft rain here. Peltin' rain. Peltin' him who fell. If he fell. *(To* ANDERSON*)* I don't know where you lie, Richard. Some field. They buried you in some field some ... For the other one, there's a cross but not close to here, no, and the name is her name on the cross which I don't think I can find, can never go back, far away, another country. *(Referring to EDDIE)* Him, her, I don't know, transformation ... Not my child anymore, not her anymore. *(To ANDERSON)* Can you help me?

ANDERSON: *(Seizing ANNIE roughly)* Choose one or it's Annie!

JOAN: Her, yes, that one. She lay on her back and she spread her legs so she could see you. She said you were thin. She said I wouldn't know you. I'd know you. I begged him, *(Referring to GEORGE)* I begged, but he wouldn't, *(Referring to ANNIE)* so she did. *(Then referring to herself in the third person)* Her, her, she listens and looks but the real colour and sound of this place escapes her and there is nothin' inside, everything's ... grey ... goin' grey ... Glowin' grey ... the sky is glowin' now!

ANNIE: I guessed you know, but I didn't give you away. You reminded me of a charmin' man I once knew, but he's gone now. They hanged him. I know that. Still ... I'm wonderin' why I didn't give you away. My brother is one of the reasons. And somethin' about you another. And I suppose I was interested in seein' what you were here for, whoever you were. I was curious, like a cat. And you could talk to me and laugh and call me Annie and kill me?

ANDERSON: If I had to.

ANNIE: Choose to. It's not them choosin', is it? It's you. Will killin' me ease the ache in your heart for your brother? Why not kill us all? Maybe that would wipe away his final terror and pain.

JOAN: You were never at Cherry Valley, were you? What's your name? Real name. Name yourself. Are you Richard or Edward? Are you someone I know?

ANNIE: Who could I kill to clear Mama's head?

JOAN: Oh don't talk of killin', talk of Talk and Namin' and Talk.

ANNIE: Why don't you choose to ride out of here?

ANDERSON: I'm not finished yet.

JOAN: Talk!

(The light is on the men.)

DANIEL:	I don't know what to say. Value to the community. I ain't done much. But I'm young, there's a lot still to come!
MAJOR:	I can't plead youth, but I'm not old.
GEORGE:	Age is to come into it then?
MAJOR:	You see here a man rich and ripe with knowledge and experience, and sharin' it all with them where I live.
GEORGE:	I'd qualify there if we were talkin' 'bout Boston.
DANIEL:	But we're not.
MAJOR:	I got the governor's ear and I'm in with the Fifty-five, and in here *(pointing to his head)* I carry details of land claims that haven't been writ, and a host of figures and sums and dealin's and doin's—and if that knowledge were lost, well—or if the power you hold through me were to go to another not so well disposed towards the Loyalist interests—
GEORGE:	I've fought for that interest.
MAJOR:	But not on the field.
GEORGE:	No. Eddie though, Eddie has! And I—I provide for the wife and daughter.
DANIEL:	Family.
GEORGE:	I'm of value to them.
DANIEL:	I'm by myself there too, but when I get buildin' I was hopin'—What about neighbours? Value to neighbours! Them on the south, I helped clear stump—
MAJOR:	I've no wife to be widowed or children orphaned, but there's a reason for that. I give my all to the state. And you gotta remember that, like the body, a state can lose fingers and toes, an arm or a leg, but if you strike at the head, the true leaders, then that state will sicken and die.
DANIEL:	And they helped me, the neighbours on the south there that I helped?
JOAN:	Look at the sky! It's startin' to turn a golden rose. At home a body'd be hearin' birds by now. Listen. Listen.
ANNIE:	Listen to me and I'll tell you something. Will you listen?

WULLIE:	I fetched thirty pound when I be sold on the block at Charleston. I be that valuable! I be so powerful you beat me and you give me the lash and you hang me for things no white man got to answer for. You be so afraid of my words, my words be taken from me and my word don't count in any case or court. I be so valuable even ole Frank Taylor cheat and lie to get my labour. How much do you think you're worth on the block, Major Williams?
GEORGE:	Eddie? You haven't said nothin' ... Speak up.
EDDIE:	If I die, you lose my Legion half-pay pension.
GEORGE:	Eddie ...
EDDIE:	What is it?
GEORGE:	You mean more than that.
EDDIE:	I went to war for you.
GEORGE:	You know how that came about.
EDDIE:	And here I am.
GEORGE:	It was the only way.
EDDIE:	That's what you said.
GEORGE:	It wasn't just for me, it was for Annie and your mother.
EDDIE:	What about Em'ly?
GEORGE:	You wanted to go! You offered to go! How else were we to survive with the English down our throats 'cause of Richard, and the Rebels at our heels 'cause of me? Was you said you'd go, you said it!
EDDIE:	I did.
GEORGE:	So don't just say the half-pay pension.
EDDIE:	Well, I was willin' to die for you then.
GEORGE:	Eddie.
EDDIE:	I'm not willin' to live for you now.
GEORGE:	Choose me! I'm an old man! I can't pull my weight! I left my life in Boston and I turned my back ... on my oldest son ... I turned my back on Richard ... and Edward. I ... Choose me.

(Dawn light continues to grow.)

JOAN: I hear you, Papa.

ANNIE: Major Anderson—Is that your real name? That was the
           name of John Andre, that most charmin' man I was tellin'
           you about who was hanged? ... I try to stop doin' that, just
           to tell things straight, but.... You get into the habit of
           butterin' up and playin' those little games with a man
           'cause you never know when you'll need one. Any one.
           And sometimes I think that I need one. And there John
           Andre was, under our roof ... and there I was, butterin'
           him up—We agree that I can be charmin'? Agreed?

JOAN: (To ANDERSON) Agreed?

ANNIE: Why do you think Major Andre took the right road held
           by the Rebels instead of the left road held by the English?

ANDERSON: I think I know why.

ANNIE: How would you know? Arnold's man told him take the
           left, I heard him.

ANDERSON: So why did he?

ANNIE: Someone told him different. Somebody convinced him.
           "Right road's less risky." "Take the right, Major." "My
           brother, Major, is fightin' with Tarleton in the south, you
           can trust me, Major." "Take the right, Major." Do you think
           a person should be held responsible for the hangin' of a
           man, a man she found charmin', 'cause she just kept sayin'
           "right" 'stead of "left"? A person could bump into an
           English regular easy as a Rebel on either road. He was a
           sweet man. I was lyin' about the trifle. A sweet man.
           Nevertheless they hanged him.

JOAN: Look at the light! It's flowin' round us and past us and
           through us! Look at your hands! (Holding up her hands) I
           can see right through the skin! I can see the bones!

           (The rose-coloured light of dawn bathes the stage.)

ANNIE: Major Andre was frightened. He knew both roads were
           risky. When I said right 'stead of left, I ... I was thinkin' of
           Arnold. Not the Arnold who betrayed the Rebel cause, but
           the Arnold who betrayed my brother Richard. Can you
           understand that?

ANDERSON: Vote!

(ANNIE *takes a paper from her pocket.*)

ANNIE: Look at this. I keep it close. I look at it sometimes. He made a copy you see, of the plans. In case he was taken. He gave it to me. He trusted me. I was to wait an hour or two after he left, and then make my way to the English. Give them the plans. I ... didn't do that. Look ... Look! ... It's the West Point plans of defense. I could've got them to the English—but I didn't. I sat in my upstairs bedroom. I looked out the window. I just held them tight in my hand. I sat there 'til supper.

ANDERSON: With the West Point plans in your hand. (*Pause*) They would have made no difference to the war.

ANNIE: Maybe they would have. Maybe they wouldn't have. I know it changed nothin' for Richard. Or Edward. Or sweet Major Andre. I wonder if he thought of me at the end ... Sometimes I feel his name fillin' my head and pressin' hard on my lips to be spoke ... There's nothin' I can do for him now. There's nothin' I can do to put paid to my brothers. Or you to put paid to yours. We oughta be lookin' to a better world for our children. That's the only way to serve our brothers.

JOAN: (*To* ANDERSON) I can see you now.

ANNIE: Go.

JOAN: (*To* ANDERSON) You can go now.

(*Pause.* JOAN *holds out her hands. A moment, then* ANDERSON *places the pistol in her hands. He exits as* ANNIE *picks up the long gun.*)

DANIEL: Hey!

MAJOR: Jump to it!

(ANNIE *covers them with the gun.*)

ANNIE: Tell them how good I am at killin' squirrels, Eddie.

EDDIE: She's good.

MAJOR: What do you think you're doin'?

ANNIE:	Not a word, Major. Take all the guns, Mama. Take them down to the water. Throw them in where it's deep and scatter the horses.

(JOAN leaves with all the guns but ANNIE's.)

MAJOR:	Have you lost your mind?
ANNIE:	I don't think so.
DANIEL:	We're saved, Major! Don't you realize that?
MAJOR:	Saved?
DANIEL:	Jesus, I was gettin' to the point of sayin' ain't none of us worth nothin'—'cept Wullie here who's worth thirty pounds, eh Wullie?
MAJOR:	Tell her to put the gun down! We gotta get out and after him, guns or no guns!
EDDIE:	What for?
MAJOR:	To capture the bugger!
ANNIE:	What's he done?
MAJOR:	Illegal detainment, kidnappin', attempted murder—!
EDDIE:	Seemed kind of a Tarleton caper for merry-makin' by an unknown soldier to me—eh Daniel?
DANIEL:	Me? ...

(He looks at ANNIE.)

ANNIE:	What do you say Daniel? If ever a man knew merry-makin' it's you.
DANIEL:	I guess 'twas—merry-making—but I'm not too happy 'bout losin' the gun, Annie. I only got but the one gun.
WULLIE:	I want you to know I'd back your charges, Major, but my word ain't worth nothin' in a court of law.
MAJOR:	George? ... *(GEORGE meets his eyes for a moment, then looks away.)* Are you all forgettin' poor Frank? The Rebel killed Frank!
DANIEL:	You come round to my way of thinkin' then, have you?
GEORGE:	If there's evidence we can swear out a warrant.

MAJOR:	We can't do nothin' standin' here! She's usin' a weapon to detain! To restrict my comin' and goin'! What's the matter with you!

(JOAN returns without the guns.)

JOAN:	I saw him!
MAJOR:	Which way did he go!
JOAN:	He rode down the path to the road with the whole string of horses behind him. He rode right into the sun! I stood there watchin' him go, and I saw him. Him and the horses. I put my hand up so? Shieldin' my eyes in order to see? And he rode on a path of light right into the sun with all of the horses behind him! And a black veil came over my eyes. When it lifted there was only the empty road. He was gone. He's gone.

(ANNIE lowers her gun.)

MAJOR:	Do you think my horse won't come for a whistle? *(Pause, he looks at each of them.)* There's sedition here. *(Starts to exit.)*
EDDIE:	Is dissent sedition?
MAJOR:	*(Stops and turns to face them)* Let me tell you something. The election slate for the Fifty-five will win! And them that's in the right camp, will prosper! You've had your chance. You all are makin' a choice right now. This country's going to flower and bloom like a rose in the wreath of Empire. It'll be built on patronage and preferment for that way's as natural as a flower turnin' its face to the sun. And if you don't find that to your likin', my advice to you is, Remove Yourself!
EDDIE:	Or remove you.

(MAJOR leaves giving a sharp whistle for his horse; the whistles continue, echoing, getting fainter and fainter. A moment, then EDDIE laughs, WULLIE joins in, they move towards the keg where EDDIE will pour drinks.)

EDDIE:	Rum all around, eh Daniel?

DANIEL:	*(Ignoring the offer as **ANNIE** moves towards the periphery of the space with **DANIEL** following her.)* You're a beautiful girl. Will you marry me, Annie?
ANNIE:	*(Laughing)* Never.

*(**GEORGE** is slowly removing the Rebel's waistcoat. He will fold it carefully, will clasp it to his chest. **JOAN** and **GEORGE** are each in their own world.)*

JOAN:	*(Examining her fingers, identifying each family member with a finger.)* Him Her Him Her Her Him.

*(**WULLIE** and **EDDIE** begin clearing the space during the dialogue; they will take down the war and Rememberin' paraphernalia and return the stage to some semblance of its virgin state at the beginning of the play. They won't leave the stage in doing so.)*

WULLIE:	Yorktown fell on October 19th.
EDDIE:	I guess so.
WULLIE:	I know so.
EDDIE:	Waxhaws was my first real engagement.
WULLIE:	I could see that. You was just a puppy at Waxhaws.
EDDIE:	Little skirmishes 'fore that.
WULLIE:	Not the same.
EDDIE:	What a couple of asses, you and me, volunteerin' for King's Mountain to get away from the Legion, eh Wullie? *(**WULLIE** laughs. **JOAN'S** attention shifts to **WULLIE** and **EDDIE**. She watches them.)* And after King's Mountain, you carried me through the swamp and the woods back to the Legion.
WULLIE:	You wasn't that heavy—for a man.
EDDIE:	Guess I wasn't. *(They stop their activity.)* You saved my life.
WULLIE:	We all be takin' turns back then.

*(Their return to work is interrupted by **JOAN**.)*

JOAN:	What happened to Em'ly?

(EDDIE looks at her mother. Pause.)

EDDIE: She's still here, Mama.

JOAN: She's gone!

EDDIE: She's changed.

JOAN: Eddie? *(Pause)* Eddie. *(She looks down at her fingers stroking lightly the four fingers of her left hand with her right. She looks back to EDDIE.)* Let me look at your face from a distance.

EDDIE: It's a new world, Mama—you gotta look up close.

JOAN: Up close?

            (She approaches EDDIE and touches her face tentatively.)

GEORGE: *(With the waistcoat pressed to his chest, in a way embracing it, referring to it and who it represents to him.)* I do love you. You know that, don't you? I love you.

JOAN: Papa? *(She looks to GEORGE.)*

EDDIE: *(To WULLIE)* I got somethin' here ... you want to see it?

WULLIE: What is it?

EDDIE: Somethin'. *(Gets out the bloody paper)* Frank was crowin' to me 'bout the thirty-nine years and I ... Here. *(Passes him the paper)*

WULLIE: He was some fella, he was. I remember him at the Waxhaws, he—*(Looks at the paper, pause)* This be Frank's copy of my indenture paper.

EDDIE: That's right.

WULLIE: How'd you get it?

EDDIE: I took it out of his pocket.

WULLIE: When?

            (Pause. EDDIE takes the paper from WULLIE, tears it up, it falls to the floor.)

JOAN: *(Whispers to GEORGE)* I can hear you. *(She takes his arm.)*

WULLIE:	*(As they return to work)* They say the army be enlistin' again.
EDDIE:	I heard that.
WULLIE:	To serve in the West Indies.
EDDIE:	Ah-huh.
WULLIE:	Are you thinkin' of joinin'?
EDDIE:	Nope ... Sierra Leone ... you ever hear of that place?
WULLIE:	Africa.
EDDIE:	They say the Loyalist Coloureds that want to go, the English'll take 'em.
WULLIE:	I heard that.
EDDIE:	You gonna go?
WULLIE:	Nope.
EDDIE:	Not gonna go?
WULLIE:	Nope.
EDDIE:	*(Laughs)* You're crazy.
WULLIE:	*(Laughs)* Yeah, that's right.

(The souvenirs and trophies have been taken down. EDDIE and WULLIE stand by the birchbark pole with their rum.)

JOAN:	I feel my feet pressin' flat 'gainst the surface of the soil now. I kneel readin' the contours of the skull and listenin' to the words spoke by the man with the missin' jawbone. The caps of my knees make a small indentation in the dirt. I see the red woman with the babe on her back step out from under the glade of trees. She holds out a bowl. She offers a bowl full of dirt. Eat, she says. Swallow. And I do.

(She slowly raises her hands, fingers spread in front of her face.)

EDDIE:	I suppose ... *(She looks up at the English flag.)*
WULLIE:	... Suppose a person could stay right here ... Try to make a place.

EDDIE: Ah-huh … A person could do that …

> *(The floor seems to glow with a dark rich swirl of colour as the lights are fading. EDDIE passes WULLIE her rum to hold as she begins slowly lowering the English flag as lights go to blackout.)*

> *Blackout*

END OF PLAY

MUSIC IN THE PLAY

THE WORLD TURNED UPSIDE DOWN

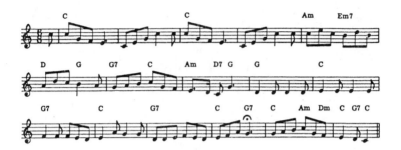

If buttercups buzzed after the bee
If boats were on land, churches on sea,
If ponies rode men, and if grass ate the corn,
And cats should be chased into holes by the mouse,
If the mammas sold their babies to gypsies for half a crown,
If summer were spring, and the other way 'round,
Then all the world would be upside down.

WHO'LL BE KING BUT CHARLIE?

Come 'round the heather,
Come over the heather,
You're welcome late and early.
Around him fling your royal king,
For who'll be the king but Charlie?

Charlie likes to kiss the girls,
Charlie likes the brandy,
Charlie likes to kiss the girls,
Whenever they come handy.

REVOLUTIONARY TEA

There was an old lady liv'd over the sea,
And she was an Island Queen.
Her daughter liv'd off in a new countrie,
With an ocean of water between.
The old lady's pockets were full of gold,
But never contented was she,
So she called on her daughter to pay her a tax,
Of three pence a pound on her tea,
Of three pence a pound on her tea.

LEATHERWING BAT

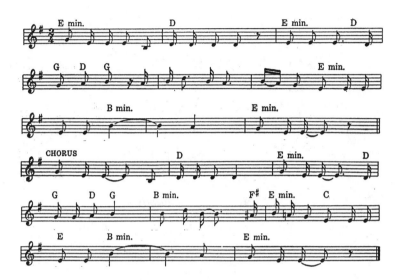

"Hi!" said the little leather-wing bat,
"I'll tell you the reason that,
The reason that I fly by night
Is because I lost my heart's delight."

Hi-di-dow, dee-diddle-um-day,
Hi-di-dow, dee-diddle-um-day,
Hi-di-dow, dee-diddle-um-day,
And a hey-lee-lee, li-lye-li-lo.

SHARON POLLOCK'S WORKS FOR THE STAGE
have been produced throughout Canada and
around the world. She is the recipient of
numerous awards recognizing excellence in
drama and is a two-time winner of the
Governor General's Literary Award for Drama
for her plays *Doc* and *Blood Relations*. Other
stage plays include *The Komagata Maru Incident;*
Generations; One Tiger to a Hill Whiskey Six
Cadenza; Death in the Family; Saucy Jack; Walsh;
Getting It Straight; The Making of Warriors;
Moving Pictures; End Dream and *Angel's*
Trumpet. Her work has been translated into
Japanese, Dutch, French and German.
Ms. Pollock resides in Calgary, Alberta.